Drug War Crimes

The Consequences of Prohibition

Drug War Crimes

The Consequences of Prohibition

Jeffrey A. Miron

The INDEPENDENT INSTITUTE

Oakland, California

The Independent Institute
100 Swan Way, Oakland, CA 94621-1428
Telephone: 510-632-1366 • Fax: 510-568-6040
Email: info@independent.org
Website: www.independent.org

ISBN: 0-945999-90-9
Cataloging-In-Publication Data available from the Library of Congress

10 9 8 7 6 5 4 3 2

The INDEPENDENT INSTITUTE

THE INDEPENDENT INSTITUTE is a non-profit, non-partisan, scholarly research and educational organization that sponsors comprehensive studies of the political economy of critical social and economic issues.

The politicization of decision-making in society has too often confined public debate to the narrow reconsideration of existing policies. Given the prevailing influence of partisan interests, little social innovation has occurred. In order to understand both the nature of and possible solutions to major public issues, The Independent Institute's program adheres to the highest standards of independent inquiry and is pursued regardless of political or social biases and conventions. The resulting studies are widely distributed as books and other publications, and are publicly debated through numerous conference and media programs. Through this uncommon independence, depth, and clarity, The Independent Institute expands the frontiers of our knowledge, redefines the debate over public issues, and fosters new and effective directions for government reform.

THE INDEPENDENT INSTITUTE
100 Swan Way, Oakland, California 94621-1428, U.S.A.
Telephone: 510-632-1366 • Facsimile: 510-568-6040
Email: info@independent.org • Website: www.independent.org

Contents

List of Illustrations

Tables

Figures

To my father, who is a libertarian,
and my mother, who is not.

1

Introduction

Drug prohibition in the United States is now almost eighty years old. Federal law first prohibited cocaine, heroin, and related drugs in 1914, and marijuana in 1937. In recent years government expenditure for prohibition enforcement has exceeded $33 billion annually, with law enforcement authorities making more than 1.5 million arrests per year on drug-related charges (Miron 2003b). In the United States, there are now more than 318,000 persons behind bars for violations of drug prohibition, more than the number of persons incarcerated for all crimes in the United Kingdom, France, Germany, Italy, and Spain combined.[1]

What does the United States gain from this incredible investment of resources? Prohibitionists believe drug use would soar if drugs were legal, and they regard any increase as undesirable per se. Prohibitionists also assert that drug use causes crime, diminishes health and productivity for drug users, encourages driving and industrial accidents, exacerbates poverty, supports terrorism, and contributes generally to societal decay. Thus, advocates claim, prohibition benefits drug users and society alike.

I argue here that drug prohibition, rather than drug use, causes most ills typically attributed to drugs. I show that prohibition's ability to reduce drug use is modest rather than dramatic, so any benefits of reduced consumption are moderate at best. I demonstrate that prohibition has a range of negative consequences, including increased violence, reduced health for drug users, transfers to criminals, and diminished civil liberties; thus, prohibition exacerbates many of the problems it allegedly solves. I explain that reduced drug use is not, in general, an appropriate goal for government policy. And I demonstrate that, even if a policy-induced reduction in drug consumption is desirable, prohibition is a terrible choice for achieving this goal.

I base these conclusions on an economic analysis of drug prohibition. This analysis uses economic reasoning to determine the likely effects of prohibition on drug use, crime, health, productivity, product quality, and other outcomes. The analysis also examines evidence on how drugs and drug policy influence each of these outcomes. There is room for scientific disagreement about some of this evidence. But dispassionate examination supports the arguments for drug legalization rather than those for prohibition.

The remainder of the book proceeds as follows.

Chapter 2 reviews the standard economic analysis of prohibition. The discussion is "positive" rather than "normative," meaning it identifies the effects of prohibition without taking a stand on whether prohibition is good or bad. The usual defense of prohibition assumes it substantially reduces drug use and, by so doing, lowers crime and improves the health and productivity of drug users. The analysis here shows, however, that prohibition-induced reductions in drug consumption are not necessarily large or even in the "desired" direction. Moreover, prohibition can increase rather than decrease crime and diminish rather than enhance health and productivity. In addition, prohibition can generate numerous undesirable consequences such as corruption, infringements on civil liberties, wealth transfers to criminals, unwarranted restrictions on medicinal uses of drugs, and insurrection in drug-producing countries. And these unintended consequences are possible even if prohibition has a substantial impact on drug use.

This positive analysis of prohibition therefore suggests two issues are central to the normative analysis of prohibition. The first is whether prohibition's effect on drug consumption is "small" or "large," and the second is whether prohibition increases or decreases crime. If the prohibition-induced change in drug consumption is small, any benefits that might result from reduced consumption are also small, implying the costs of prohibition almost certainly exceed the benefits. If prohibition increases rather than decreases crime, then it causes one of the main problems it attempts to alleviate, raising questions about prohibition even if it substantially reduces drug use. Thus, these two issues deserve special attention.

Chapter 3 addresses the effect of prohibition on drug consumption by examining cirrhosis death rates during the Prohibition period. Although not identical to current drug prohibition in structure or enforcement, alcohol prohibition is a natural laboratory for studying the effects of drug prohibition on drug consumption. Debates over prohibition routinely cite this episode as supporting one side or the other, but previous analyses have not controlled adequately for factors other than prohibition that might have influenced cirrhosis. The analysis here indicates alcohol prohibition had a modest effect on alcohol consumption, which implies drug prohibition has a modest effect on drug use. Auxiliary evidence from a variety of sources suggests the same conclusion.

Chapter 4 examines the effect of drug prohibition on violence. Prohibition advocates claim drug use causes violent behavior, while prohibition critics claim prohibition generates violence by forcing drug markets underground. These claims are not mutually exclusive, but it is important to determine if one or the other predominates in practice. The chapter addresses these competing claims by first examining homicide rates over the past century in the United States. The evidence that alcohol prohibition had a modest impact on alcohol consumption suggests drug prohibition has a modest impact in reducing violence, but this evidence is not by itself decisive. The chapter shows that both drug and alcohol prohibition coincided with increases in the homicide rate, consistent with the view that under prohibition, market participants substitute guns for lawyers in the resolution of disputes. The chapter then discusses the relation between prohibition and violence across countries. Again, the evidence indicates that vigorous enforcement of prohibition is associated with higher rather than lower rates of violence, contrary to the standard defenses of prohibition. And a broad range of other evidence is consistent with this conclusion.

In Chapters 5 and 6, I turn from the positive analysis of drug prohibition to the "normative" analysis, meaning the question of whether prohibition is desirable policy. The implication of Chapters 2–4 is that prohibition has numerous effects, beyond any decrease in drug consumption, including increased violence, greater corruption, diminished health for users, reduced civil liberties, and more. These effects are all undesirable, so the question is whether these consequences are worth paying in exchange for whatever reduction in drug consumption prohibition achieves.

Chapter 5 addresses this question by discussing under what conditions reduced drug consumption is an appropriate goal of public policy. Most policy discussions take as given that reduced drug consumption is beneficial, but this assumption does not follow from standard economic principles. Reduced drug consumption might be an appropriate goal if drug consumption generates externalities or if consumer choices about drug consumption are myopic, but the evidence shows that externalities from drugs, and myopia with respect to drugs, are both modest relative to exaggerated fear stories promulgated by prohibitionists. Moreover, neither externalities nor myopia related to drugs are obviously different from those of many legal goods. In any case, policies to reduce drug consumption make sense only if their benefits exceed their costs. Since prohibition has substantial enforcement costs and itself generates externalities, prohibition is a poor choice for reducing drug consumption.

Chapter 6 therefore asks what policy toward drugs achieves the best balancing of costs and benefits. Many modifications of current prohibition, such as diminished enforcement, decriminalization, medicalization, or legalization of marijuana only, are moves in a beneficial direction, but they are inferior to a regime in which drugs are legal. Within a legal regime, policies such as subsidized treatment, needle exchanges, public health campaigns, age restrictions, or limits on advertising might have desirable effects, but these policies also have negative consequences that can outweigh any positives. The bottom line is that legalization, with drugs treated like all other commodities, is the best policy for society overall.

Note

1. The exact number of U.S. drug prisoners was 318,189 in 2000; see Office of National Drug Control Policy (2003), Table 33. The exact number for the European countries was 300,675 in 2000; see Barclay and Tavares (2002), Table 3.

2

The Economic Analysis of Drug Prohibition

This chapter reviews the standard economic analysis of drug prohibition, with two main messages in mind. The first is that prohibition's ability to reduce drug consumption is modest rather than dramatic, contrary to claims typically made by prohibition advocates. The second message is that, whether or not prohibition substantially reduces drug use, prohibition has numerous other effects, most of them undesirable.[1]

Prices and Quantities under Prohibition: Supply

The most obvious effect of prohibition is to raise some costs of supplying drugs. Under prohibition, suppliers face legal punishments for manufacturing, distributing, and selling drugs. Equivalently, black market suppliers incur the costs of bribing law enforcement authorities and elected officials so as to avoid these legal punishments. The magnitude of these effects depends on the level of enforcement; weakly imposed prohibitions raise costs less than more stringently imposed prohibitions. Likewise, the degree to which prohibition allows exceptions (such as the medicinal use of drugs) affects the degree to which it promotes a black market and raises costs.

The increased costs created by prohibition imply that, other things equal, drug prices are higher, and drug consumption is lower, under prohibition. Other things are not likely to be equal, however, so the net effects of prohibition on costs, price, and consumption are more subtle.

To begin, black market suppliers of drugs can easily evade government regulations and taxes, including environmental regulations, employment discrimination laws, child-labor laws, antitrust laws, occupational health and safety regulations, tariffs and other import restrictions, income taxes, social security taxes, and excise taxes. These cost savings offset some of the increased costs caused by prohibition, implying a weaker effect on costs and price. Because firms in a legal market can always evade taxes (by acting as if their product were prohibited), costs and price under prohibition can never be lower than they would be in a legal market. But they need not be much higher.

A second reason prohibition might have a weak effect on costs is that increased expenditure for enforcement of prohibition can imply decreased expenditure for enforcement of other cost-increasing government policies. For example, expenditure for enforcement of prohibition might lead to diminished expenditure for enforcement of an excise tax on drugs, implying a small overall effect on costs. Thus, governments might choose prohibition over other policies because prohibition appears to cost nothing; this implies expenditure for enforcement of cost-increasing policies might actually be lower under prohibition.

A related reason prohibition might have a weak effect on costs is that the efficacy of enforcement expenditure is plausibly greater for taxation and regulation policies than for prohibition. Taxes and regulations create potential complainants who monitor businesses subject to these polices. These complainants include employees (labor market regulation, OSHA regulation), customers (false or misleading advertising), consumer watchdog groups (environmental regulation), and rival firms (most cost-increasing policies, including taxation). Prohibition creates no such complainants; indeed, prohibition outlaws mutually beneficial exchange between drug buyers and sellers. Prohibition enforcement must therefore rely on informants, sting operations, busts, and the like, all of which require enforcement expenditure. And the groups that might complain about noncompliance with tax and regulatory policies in a legal market are unlikely to complain in a black market, since this creates legal risks for the complainant. These considerations suggest that, for a given level of enforcement expenditure, the costs imposed by enforcement of a given policy are higher in a legal as opposed to an illicit market.

A third reason prohibition might have modest effects on costs is that prohibition affects the ability to advertise. In legal markets, advertising comprises a substantial fraction of the price of many goods. In a prohibited market, firms face increased costs of advertising, since such activities reveal their identity or location. This higher cost of advertising, in and of itself, suggests higher prices under prohibition, but there are indirect effects that might yield lower prices. If advertising enhances product differentiation, as with alcohol, cigarettes, or soft drinks, then advertising can make demand less sensitive to price. In this case, the de facto prohibition on advertising that occurs under prohibition means less advertising, *more* price-sensitive demands, and lower prices.

Additionally, advertising in many industries mainly divides a fixed pie of consumers among different firms rather than attracting new consumers. In these industries advertising is like an arms race. Each firm advertises to attract consumers from other firms, but each ends up with approximately the same market share. Worse, from the firm perspective, each has higher total costs due to advertising, so price is higher and consumption is lower. Firms in this situation would prefer not to advertise, but an agreement to do so would violate antitrust laws. Prohibition, however, effectively bans advertising, lowers industry costs, and increases the size of the industry.

A final factor that affects price under prohibition is prohibition's impact on market power. One possibility is that prohibition facilitates evasion of antitrust laws, thereby increasing market power. Another is that prohibition lowers the marginal cost of violence, since drug traffickers are already evading law enforcement authorities. This means suppliers have an easier time maintaining collusive agreements because the parties can, literally, threaten to kill defectors. If these are the predominant effects of prohibition on market power, prices should be higher by more than the increase in direct costs.

On the other hand, certain enforcement activities appear to enhance competition. The arrest and incarceration of a dominant supplier can encourage price wars among remaining suppliers as they attempt to capture the arrested supplier's market share. Increased enforcement can make it harder for firms to observe their rivals' prices, which inhibits the ability to collude. In addition, enforcement can make it profitable to incur the fixed costs of new distribution networks or new evasion techniques, which then compete with existing arrangements. For example, government efforts to prevent Peruvian coca paste from being transported to Colombia for processing into cocaine caused Colombian processors to develop coca-growing capabilities in Colombia. Thus, the net effect of prohibition on market power is ambiguous and probably depends on both the level and kind of enforcement activities.

All of these considerations suggest rethinking the view that prohibition substantially raises the costs of supplying drugs. The overall effect is almost certainly to increase costs and thus price, but the magnitude of the increase is not obviously large on a priori grounds and must be determined empirically. Chapter 3 presents evidence based on prohibitions of alcohol, cocaine, and heroin in the United States.

Prices and Quantities Under Prohibition: Demand

In addition to affecting the supply side of the market, prohibition affects the demand side. Prohibition reduces the demand for drugs by imposing legal penalties for possession and by increasing uncertainty about product quality. Further, prohibition decreases demand if consumers exhibit "respect for the law." At the same time, prohibition can increase demand by creating a "forbidden fruit."

As with the supply side, the magnitude of the change in demand caused by prohibition depends on the nature of the law and on the degree to which it is enforced. In some cases prohibition does not impose penalties for possession of small quantities of drugs, and in many cases the penalties that exist are weakly enforced.

The degree to which prohibition in the United States imposes penalties for purchase or possession is arguably lax. Although there are more than 1.2 million possession arrests each year, there are more than 28 million drug users, and most purchase drugs on many occasions.[2] Thus, the most obvious calculation—the number of arrests divided by the number of drug purchases—suggests low probabilities of arrest for mere purchase or possession. Moreover, many arrests for possession occur because the arrestee violated some other law—prostitution, theft, speeding, loitering, disorderly conduct, and so on—and was also found to possess drugs. Thus, otherwise law-abiding citizens who wish to purchase and consume drugs face minimal risk of arrest or other sanction.

The effect of prohibition on the demand for drugs also depends on the degree to which consumers substitute between illegal drugs and legal commodities such as alcohol. If drug consumers view non-prohibited goods as close substitutes for illegal drugs, prohibition-induced increases in drug prices cause substantial declines in drug consumption but corresponding increases in other-goods consumption. If drug consumers view legal and illegal goods as complements, then prohibition-induced increases in drug prices reduce consumption of both kinds of goods. The existing evidence is not definitive, but it suggests a moderate degree of substitution between illegal drugs and legal goods, especially alcohol.[3]

The bottom line of this discussion is that prohibition plausibly reduces drug consumption relative to what would occur under laissez-faire, but the magnitude of this reduction is not necessarily large. A related issue is that a priori reasoning does not pin down whether prohibition mainly affects casual or heavy consumption. Both of these questions are critical to the evaluation of prohibition, as discussed further in Chapter 5.

Prohibition and Crime

In addition to affecting the price and quantity of drug consumption, prohibition has many other effects. Perhaps the most important are its effects on crime.

Prohibition affects crime via several mechanisms. Participants in an illegal market cannot use the legal and judicial system to resolve disputes, so they seek other methods such as violence. Reinforcing this tendency is the fact that violent acts are less costly to participants in a prohibited market because evading apprehension for violation of drug laws is complementary with evading apprehension for initiating violence. As with prohibition's effect on the price and quantity of drugs, prohibition's effect on crime depends not just on the existence of prohibition but on the specifics of the law and the degree to which it is enforced. Chapter 4 addresses this issue in more detail.

Prohibition can encourage violent and nonviolent crime by shifting criminal justice resources away from deterrence of nonprohibition crimes toward prohibition enforcement. For example, when police, prosecutors, and judges spend their time pursuing drug users and sellers, they have less time to pursue murderers, rapists, and the like.[4] Similarly, locking up drug offenders leaves less room in prisons for other offenders and encourages the early release of violent criminals.

Prohibition can also increase income-generating crime, such as theft or prostitution, to the extent prohibition raises the prices of illegal drugs. Assuming some drug users earn their income from crime, higher prices require increased crime to finance a given quantity of drug consumption. It is unclear to what degree this effect has operated in the United States over the past several decades, since drug prices have fallen substantially while enforcement has risen several fold (Basov, Jacobson, and Miron 2001). And the high correlation between drug use and crime does not determine to what degree prohibition causes crime; the observed correlation partially indicates that some criminals also use drugs (Greenberg and Adler 1974).[5] There is suggestive evidence, however, that higher drug prices are associated with higher rates of income-generating crime.[6]

A different way prohibition increases crime is by weakening respect for the law. Experience to date indicates that even with substantial enforcement, tens of millions of persons continue to sell, purchase, and consume drugs. The vast majority of such persons, however, pay little penalty for their lawbreaking, so they are emboldened by this experience and become more likely to break other laws. Those who do not violate prohibition realize that others are doing so with impunity, and this makes them less law-abiding as well. Thus, prohibition fosters a social norm in which voluntary compliance with all laws is diminished and hence crime rates in general are high.

Prohibition also fosters corruption of police, prosecutors, judges, and politicians. This occurs because lawsuits, lobbying, and campaign contributions do not exist in a prohibited industry. In addition, drug traffickers have high profits to protect and thus added incentive to bribe or threaten those who might impede these profits. Evidence on the magnitude of corruption is difficult to obtain, but anecdotal evidence of drug-trade-induced corruption is abundant (e.g., U.S. General Accounting Office 1998; ACLU-Texas 2003).

The effects of prohibition in generating crime and corruption can extend to other countries, especially if the United States pressures drug-producing countries to enforce prohibition.[7] Beyond the standard violence- and corruption-producing effects discussed above, prohibition can promote civil unrest by providing income to rebel groups such as the Shining Path in Peru, the FARC in Colombia, or the Taliban in Afghanistan. Under prohibition, these groups sell protection services to drug traffickers.[8] Thus, prohibition (rather than drug use) supports terrorism.

The hypothesis that drug prohibition causes crime contrasts with the claim often made by prohibition advocates that drug use itself causes crime (e.g., by reducing inhibitions or exacerbating aggressiveness). Chapter 4 examines the evidence that prohibition causes violent crime. It is useful to note here, however, that the evidence for a causal effect of drug use on crime does not stand up to careful scrutiny.

The standard "evidence" for a causal effect consists of statistics that document a high frequency of drug use among arrestees. For example, U.S. Department of Justice (2003) documents that in the thirty-five cities monitored in 2000, at least 50 percent of adult male arrestees tested positive for one or more illicit drugs.

These statistics document that many criminals use drugs, but they do not demonstrate that drug use causes criminal behavior. First, the correlation between drug use and crime is contaminated by the fact that many arrests are for drug possession. It is hardly surprising that people arrested for drug possession also use drugs, but this fact shows that drug use "causes" crime only in a tautological sense. Second, these data provide no evidence that drug users were under the influence of drugs at the time they committed their crimes—and even if they were under the influence, that does not mean the influence was to make them criminogenic.[9] Third, existing data also suggest that a substantial percentage of criminals consumed alcohol before commission of their crimes, so at a minimum the standard evidence does not indicate which substance is implicated.[10]

Beyond these problems, the fact that many criminals are also drug users shows merely that drug use is correlated with criminal behavior. The methodology used in these analyses would also demonstrate that consumption of fast food or wearing blue jeans causes criminal behavior. If people from particular socioeconomic groups engage in a range of illicit behavior, then one will find a correlation between drug and non-drug crime independent of any effect of drug use on criminal behavior. Stated differently, the set of arrestees is not a random sample of the population. Data on arrestees do not indicate how many people consume drugs without engaging in criminal behavior (other than drug possession itself) and thus say nothing about the tendency of drug use to cause such behavior.

Finally, reviews of the literature on drug use and crime have consistently concluded there is little evidence that drug use causes crime.[11] For example, Fagan (1993) concludes that "there is little evidence that alcohol or drugs directly cause violence" and that "several reviewers have concluded that alcohol is the substance most likely to lead to psychopharmacological violence," although "there is some evidence that cocaine, barbiturates, amphetamines, phencyclidine (PCP), and steroids also have psychopharmacological properties that can motive violence." He also notes that "the most consistent and predictable relationship between substances and violence is a result of trafficking in illicit drugs." Thus, the evidence that purports to show a causal effect of drug use on crime shows no such thing.

Other Effects of Drug Prohibition

Beyond the effects on price, quantity, and crime, prohibition has a number of other effects.

Prohibition inhibits quality control in the market for drugs because consumers cannot easily sue drug sellers or complain to government agencies about faulty merchandise. This does not necessarily mean quality is low under prohibition; even black market producers have an incentive to generate repeat business by giving customers a good deal (see Haworth and Simpson 2004). But the costs of advertising are extreme in a prohibited market, which makes it hard for suppliers to establish a reputation for quality. This uncertainty about product quality suggests an elevated frequency of overdoses and accidental poisonings under prohibition.

A number of examples illustrate this point. During Prohibition, deaths due to alcoholism rose relative to other proxies for alcohol consumption, presumably because consumption of adulterated alcohol increased (Miron and Zwiebel 1991). Indeed, federal regulation required manufacturers of industrial alcohol to adulterate their product, knowing that much would be diverted to illegal consumption (Merz 1931). In one case, an adulterant used by bootleggers to disguise alcohol as medicine turned out to cause permanent paralysis, victimizing thousands (Morgan 1982). Similarly, the chemical Paraquat (dipyridylium), which the U.S. government encouraged Mexico to spray on marijuana fields, sickened many consumers (Duke and Gross 1993: 195).

Under legalization, the incidence of accidental poisonings or overdoses would not be zero, just as it is not zero for currently legal goods such as alcohol. But the rate of such incidents would decline significantly, since consumers would know the potency of the drugs they consume and have far greater confidence that the drugs contained the desired ingredients rather than unknown contaminants.[12]

Because suppliers under prohibition need to hide their activities from the authorities, traffickers have an incentive to produce and ship drugs in the most concentrated and hence most easily concealed form (e.g., crack versus cocaine, heroin versus opium, spirits versus beer). This implies prohibition expands the availability of potent forms of drugs or even helps create those more potent forms. This does not necessarily change the manner in which drug consumption takes place; consumers can dilute the drugs they purchase to achieve a lower degree of potency. Moreover, high-potency products typically exist in legal markets (e.g., 151 Rum). In a black market, however, it is difficult for consumers to determine potency, so the combination of high and uncertain potency implies an elevated frequency of accidental overdoses.

A different consequence of drug prohibition is increased transmission of HIV, hepatitis, and other blood-borne diseases. Prohibition raises drug prices, which encourages injection because this ingestion method produces a high "bang-for-the-buck." This factor, combined with prohibition-induced restrictions on clean needles, means more needle sharing and increased transmission of blood-borne diseases. In a legal market with lower prices, most consumers would smoke, snort, eat, or drink drugs like cocaine or heroin, even though these ingestion methods are less "efficient" than injection.[13] Alternatively, producers in a legal market might package drugs with disposable syringes, which would reduce the incentive to share needles.

A further effect of drug prohibition is the transfer of wealth to criminals. Prohibition requires government expenditure for enforcement, which means higher taxes or reduced expenditure on other government programs. In addition, drug suppliers do not pay taxes on their illicit income, nor do governments collect sales or excise taxes in prohibited markets. Thus, under prohibition the members of society most willing to break the law gain at the expense of society generally. Indeed, since prohibition gives violent persons a comparative advantage they would not otherwise enjoy, prohibition enriches a particularly undeserving element of society.

The magnitude of this wealth transfer is substantial. In 2000, the latest year for which data are available, total revenue in the illicit drug trade was about $64 billion (Office of National Drug Control Policy 2001: 3). Assuming an average tax rate of 30 percent, this implies a $21 billion transfer to criminals every year. These estimates use current prices of illegal drugs to calculate the size of the illicit drug sector, but under legalization, prices would be lower. In that case, the tax revenue would be less than $21 billion. Policy might obtain an amount close to this, however, using sin taxation. In addition, there is still a transfer to criminals under current policy, but some of it is from drug consumers to drug producers.

Because several illegal drugs are grown or manufactured abroad, U.S. prohibition affects relations with these countries. For example, our government's desire to arrest drug traffickers who have crossed into Mexico has angered Mexican citizens over what they regard as infringements on Mexico's sovereignty. Similarly, U.S. demands for extradition of drug lords have generated conflict with

Colombia (Thoumi 1995). And the United States has pressured Mexico and Colombia into enforcing their own prohibition laws more rigorously to reduce smuggling of drugs into the United States or to eliminate prohibition-induced corruption (Toro 1995).[14]

Prohibition also changes accepted definitions of civil liberties and encourages modifications of criminal justice enforcement. In contrast to crimes such as murder, assault, burglary, or rape, drug crimes do not produce natural complainants. For this reason, enforcement of prohibition requires tactics that are more invasive than those used to address other crimes. For example, Baum (1992: 888) writes that Supreme Court decisions

> in the past decade let police obtain search warrants on the strength of anonymous tips ... [and] did away with the need for warrants when the police want to search luggage, trash cans, car interiors, bus passengers, fenced private property and barns.... [The Court] let prosecutors hold defendants without bail.... It permitted the confiscation of property before a suspect is charged.... It let prosecutors imprison people twice ... for the same crime.... It allowed seizure of defense attorney's legal fees in drug cases.... [And] it let stand a sentence of mandatory life without parole for simple drug possession.

These effects are inevitable products of attempts to enforce laws against victimless crimes.[15]

An additional consequence of drug prohibition is increased racial tension. Prohibition is a victimless crime, so enforcement must use aggressive and subjective tactics such as racial profiling, in which police, customs agents, and other law enforcement authorities stop and search minorities to a disproportionate degree. The vast majority of persons stopped or searched have not been linked to any crime, so the potential to inflame racial hostility is obvious.

Prohibition also fosters aggressive enforcement tactics like asset seizure and forfeiture.[16] Under current law, federal and state law enforcement authorities can seize and forfeit cash, bank accounts, houses, land, cars, boats, airplanes, and other assets that they suspect of "facilitating" drug crimes. The assets can be seized even if the suspect is acquitted, and the owner must prove the property was not used to facilitate a drug crime. Most importantly, the local police in most states keep a substantial fraction of the proceeds from these forfeitures, which encourages enforcement of drug laws rather than deterrence of other crime.[17] It also makes local police departments to some degree self-financing, reducing their accountability.[18]

A different policy fostered by prohibition is mandatory minimum sentences. Mandatory minimums predate drug prohibition and exist for other crimes, but most such sentences are for drug law violations (U.S. Sentencing Commission 1991). These minimums cause distorted incentives for prosecutors and unjust outcomes for drug defendants. For example, small fry have little to trade in the way of names or assets, so they sometimes get harsher sentences than bigger fish who can plea-bargain more effectively.[19]

The desire to enforce drug prohibition has likewise spawned a substantial and costly anti–money laundering effort to track the financial flows associated with the illegal drug trade. Under these laws, banks, financial intermediaries, and other businesses are responsible for substantial record keeping and must report "suspicious" transactions to law enforcement authorities (U.S. Department of Treasury 2000a). The history of these laws and the attempts to enforce them suggest suppliers consistently develop mechanisms for avoiding the impact of any new regulation or enforcement. Thus, the laws increase costs on financial intermediaries but have little impact on drug suppliers.[20]

Another effect of prohibition is reduced use of marijuana and opiates for medical purposes. Marijuana is classified by the Controlled Substances Act as a Schedule I drug, which means it cannot be prescribed under any circumstance. This classification treats marijuana identically to heroin and LSD, and more restrictively than morphine, cocaine, and many other potent medications.

Whether marijuana is superior to alternative medications or treatments is not yet fully determined, mainly because prohibition makes it difficult for researchers to conduct appropriate scientific studies. Nevertheless, some scientific evidence suggests that marijuana provides relief from nausea, pain, and muscle spasms and that it alleviates symptoms of glaucoma, epilepsy, multiple sclerosis, AIDS, and migraine headaches, among other ailments.[21] In addition, abundant anecdotal evidence is consistent with these claims (Grinspoon and Bakalar 1993). Indeed, the Food and Drug Administration has approved the use of Marinol, a synthetic version of the most important ingredient in marijuana (THC), for treating nausea induced by chemotherapy.

Most opiates used in medical practice are Schedule II or III drugs, which means doctors can legally prescribe them under appropriate conditions.[22] Prohibition nevertheless fosters a climate in which doctors worry about legal or regulatory penalties for "overprescribing" and therefore undertreat the alleviation of pain.[23]

Beyond all these effects, prohibition requires substantial government expenditure. In recent years this expenditure has exceeded $33 billion in the United States (Miron 2003b). This is well below the costs of the largest government programs, such as national defense, but still a major commitment of resources.

Summary

The analysis above shows that drug prohibition has a broad range of effects. Among all the effects, however, two stand out as critical: the impact on drug consumption, and the effect on violence. If, as argued by proponents, prohibition substantially reduces drug consumption and violence, the policy cannot be dismissed out of hand. If, as suggested above, prohibition reduces consumption only moderately and increases violence, then the policy is highly suspect although not necessarily undesirable under all circumstances. These two empirical issues are thus particularly important to the evaluation of prohibition. The next two chapters examine the evidence.

Notes

1. The analysis draws heavily on Miron and Zwiebel (1995) and Miron (1998, 2001a, 2003a). For an excellent overview of the costs of prohibition see also the short paper by Mishan (2001).

2. The total number of drug arrests is from *Sourcebook of Criminal Justice Statistics Online,* Table 4.1, accessed at http://www.albany.edu/sourcebook/1995/pdf/t41.pdf, 9 August 2003. The percent of arrests for possession is from *Uniform Crime Reports,* Table 4.1, accessed at http://www.fbi.gov/ucr/cius_02/pdf/4sectionfour.pdf, 3 December 2003. The number of drug users is for past year use in 2001 from the National Household Survey on Drug Abuse, Table H.2, accessed at http://www.samhsa.gov/oas/NHSDA/2klNHSDA/vol2/appendixh_1.htm#tableh.1, 9 August 2003.

3. In *Licit and Illicit Drugs,* Edward M. Breecher (1972) provides numerous examples of substitution; see pages 8–11, 85, 185, 277, and 400 and Chapters 55 and 59. Feldman (1927) provides anecdotal evidence that opiate consumption increased during the first few years of alcohol prohibition, while Apsler and Harding (1991) document that patients in drug-treatment programs increase their marijuana and alcohol consumption as their opiate consumption declines. See also Conlin, Dickert-Conlin, and Pepper (2002) and the discussion provided therein.

4. See Benson, Rasmussen, and Kim (1998); Benson et al. (1992); and Sollars, Benson, and Rasmussen (1994) for evidence consistent with such an effect.

5. For work that documents a correlation between drug use and property crime, see, for example, Ball et al. (1981, 1982); Ball, Shaffer, and Nurco (1983); and Anglin and Speckart (1988).

6. See Brown and Silverman (1974, 1980); Silverman and Spruill (1977).

7. See, for example, Atkins (1998); Lerner (1998); Melo (1998); and Toro (1998) concerning Bolivia, Peru, Colombia, and Mexico, respectively.

8. McClintock (1988) discusses the fact that American drug-prohibition efforts cemented a relation between Peruvian drug traffickers and the Shining Path during the 1980s.

9. For example, Bennett and Wright (1984) report the results of interviews with burglary offenders, many of whom report that they had consumed

alcohol before committing their offense and that they had committed their offense under the influence of alcohol. But most saw no causal relation; these offenders suggested they sometimes planned their offenses while in drinking situations or just drank a lot generally.

10. See Greenfeld (1998); National Institute of Justice (2003). Indeed, some studies suggest, if anything, a higher correlation between alcohol consumption and crime than between drug use and crime. See Dawkins (1997); Wieczorek, Welte, and Abel (1990); U.S. Department of Justice (1999).

11. See, for example, Duke and Gross (1993), 37–42, 53–54, 64–66, 73–74; and U.S. Department of Justice (1992), 5.

12. A related issue is that prohibition increases infrequent, heavy consumption and discourages frequent, casual consumption, since this reduces the risk of arrest.

13. See National Research Council (1995) for discussion of these issues.

14. See also Palmer (1992); Craig (1981); Bagley (1988a, 1988b, 1988c); Tokatlian (1988); Falco (1995); Lowenfeld (1989, 1990a, 1990b, 1991).

15. See Wisotsky (1992) or Gray (2001), Chapter 3, for a more detailed discussion of these issues.

16. See Blumenson and Nilsen (1998) for a more detailed discussion of the issues raised here.

17. Under the Comprehensive Crime Act of 1984, federal authorities began the process of "adopting" state and local seizures so that the seized assets would flow back to law enforcement agencies, circumventing laws in some states requiring that the proceeds of such seizures go to general state coffers or specific other uses, such as education.

18. Mast, Benson, and Rasmussen (1998) provide suggestive evidence that the opportunity to reap the financial benefits of assets seizures has tilted state and local law enforcement toward increased enforcement of drug crimes. See also Benson and Rasmussen (1996) and Boudreaux and Pritchard (1997).

19. Schlosser (1994a, 1994b) discusses the injustices created by mandatory minimum sentences and the desire to prosecute drug offenders.

20. Andelman (1994) provides an overview and history of drug suppliers' attempts to launder money and government attempts to prevent that laundering by increasing regulation and enforcement.

21. See Institute of Medicine (1999) for further discussion of these issues.

22. Heroin is an exception to this statement, since it is a Schedule I drug.

23. For discussion of these issues, see Hill (1993); Henneberger (1994);

American Academy of Pain Medicine and the American Pain Society (1997); Sullum (1997); Joranson and Gilson (1998); Joranson et al. (2000).

3

The Effect of Drug Prohibition on Drug Consumption: Evidence from Alcohol Prohibition

Analyzing the effect of drug prohibition on drug use is difficult because the data necessary for such an investigation are limited and low quality (National Research Council 2001; Horowitz 2001). The ideal evidence on this issue compares drug use across time periods with and without prohibition, or across countries with and without prohibition, controlling for other relevant determinants of drug use. In practice, this approach is virtually impossible, since reliable data on drug use do not exist before the onset of U.S. drug prohibition in 1914, and all countries currently prohibit drugs to some degree. Thus, examining the impact of prohibition on drug consumption is problematic.[1]

One useful piece of evidence, however, is the U.S. experience with prohibition of alcohol, which occurred from 1920 through 1933. Although current U.S. drug prohibition is not identical to alcohol prohibition, the similarities are substantial in terms of the commodity prohibited and the prohibition regime imposed. In addition, cirrhosis death rates constitute a good proxy for the consumption of alcohol, and some data exist on alcohol prices during Prohibition. A broad array of researchers has therefore examined this period in the attempt to infer drug prohibition's impact on drug consumption.[2]

This section examines the effect of Prohibition on cirrhosis death rates, and it discusses the implications for current drug prohibition. The analysis draws heavily on Dills and Miron (2003), which contains a more detailed and technical treatment of the issues involved. Since the technical and nontechnical approaches yield similar conclusions, it suffices to present the simpler and less technical versions of the results. The bottom line is that Prohibition appears to have reduced cirrhosis death rates by 10–20 percent. This is not a trivial effect, but it is far smaller than suggested by many advocates of prohibition.

Alcohol Prohibition and Cirrhosis

Reliable data on the consumption of alcohol during Prohibition are not available. To remedy this problem, analyses typically consider data on cirrhosis of the liver, which is plausibly a good proxy for alcohol consumption.[3] For example, Merck & Co (1992: 890) states that "in general, a linear correlation exists between the intensity of alcohol abuse in terms of duration and dose and the development of liver disease."

The use of cirrhosis to measure alcohol consumption is not without difficulties, however. One issue is that cirrhosis is probably a better proxy for heavy alcohol consumption than for moderate or light alcohol consumption. This characteristic of cirrhosis is not a severe limitation, since heavy consumption of alcohol or drugs is the main focus of policies directed at these goods. A second problem is that cirrhosis typically develops only after years of alcohol consumption; thus, a change in alcohol consumption might not cause an immediate change in the cirrhosis death rate. This issue is more relevant for increases as opposed to decreases in cirrhosis; reduced alcohol consumption leads to reduced risk of cirrhosis almost immediately because the liver is able to regenerate partially if alcohol consumption stops. Increased alcohol consumption, however, leads to increased risk of cirrhosis only with a lag. These caveats do not invalidate using cirrhosis as a proxy for alcohol consumption, but they suggest careful interpretation of the data.[4]

Figure 3.1 presents data on the death rate from cirrhosis for the period 1900–1997. The data show that cirrhosis was substantially lower after the onset of national prohibition (in January 1920) than it had been in most of the pre-Prohibition period. The death rate declined from 12–14 deaths per year per 100,000 population during the 1910–1915 period to 7–7.5 during the Prohibition period. This is the fact typically cited as indicating Prohibition caused a substantial decline in alcohol consumption.[5] Setting aside for the moment what constitutes a "substantial" reduction, closer examination raises doubts about the conclusion that Prohibition caused the low level of cirrhosis during the 1920–1933 period.

Figure 3.1
U.S. cirrhosis death rate, 1900-1997 (per 100,000)

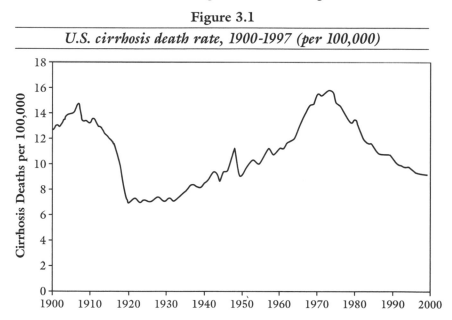

As can be seen more easily in Figure 3.2, which isolates data for the 1910–1940 period, the cirrhosis death rate was already at its minimum level when Prohibition took effect in January 1920. This does not necessarily mean Prohibition had no effect; it is possible cirrhosis would have risen after 1920 had Prohibition not occurred. But Prohibition did not cause the decline in cirrhosis from its level in the early 1910s to its level in 1920, so the low level in the 1920s is not by itself evidence of Prohibition's efficacy in reducing cirrhosis.

Figure 3.2

U.S. cirrhosis death rates, 1910-1940 (per 100,000)

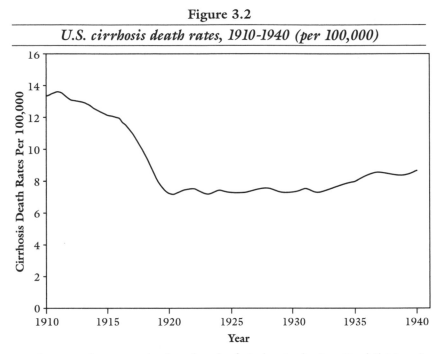

A second reason the low level of cirrhosis during Prohibition is not necessarily due to Prohibition is that the data do not show a sudden or dramatic increase in cirrhosis after repeal in 1934. Instead, cirrhosis increases only gradually over several decades, and cirrhosis declines substantially starting around 1970, well after Prohibition ended.

A possible response to this last argument is that even if alcohol consumption increased substantially after repeal, it would have taken many years for this increase to raise the death rate from cirrhosis. This hypothesis is unconvincing, however, for several reasons. First, it suggests that even if cirrhosis did not jump in 1934, it should have jumped, say, ten years later in (lagged) response to the jump in alcohol consumption. Such a jump is not evident in Figure 3.1. Second, this hypothesis is inconsistent with data on admittances to hospitals for alcohol psychosis and on deaths due to alcoholism (Miron and Zwiebel 1991); these two series are likely related to alcohol consumption with shorter lags than cirrhosis.

Third, the hypothesis implies that during the first years after repeal, the amount of cirrhosis relative to alcohol consumption should have been unusually low; setting aside the first year or two after repeal, when official statistics almost certainly understate alcohol consumption, this is not apparent in the data.

Although the raw data do not show that prohibition reduced cirrhosis, a complete analysis must consider a range of factors to determine what cirrhosis would have done in the absence of prohibition. In particular, it is useful to determine what caused the large decline in cirrhosis in the decade before national prohibition.

Table 3.1

States passing state-level prohibitions before federal prohibition

Before 1900	Kansas, Maine, New Hampshire, North Dakota
1907	Georgia, Oklahoma
1908	Alabama, Mississippi, North Carolina
1909	Tennessee
1912	West Virginia
1914	Arizona, Colorado, Oregon, Virginia, Washington
1915	Alabama, Arkansas, Idaho, Iowa, South Carolina
1916	Michigan, Montana, Nebraska, South Dakota
1917	Indiana, New Hampshire, New Mexico, Utah
1918	Florida, Nevada, Ohio, Wyoming
1919	Kentucky, Texas

Notes: New Hampshire repealed its 1855 prohibition in 1903.
Alabama repealed its 1908 prohibition in 1911.

Source: Wickersham, v.5 (1931, pp. 640–641)

One factor to consider is state-level prohibitions of alcohol, which were adopted at an increasing rate during the 1910–1920 period. Table 3.1 shows the states adopting state-level prohibition in each year over the 1900–1920 period. These data seem to suggest state prohibitions contributed to the decrease in cirrhosis during the 1910s, since the number of prohibitions increased substantially around the time cirrhosis decreased.

Several factors, however, cast doubt on this hypothesis. Although the number of states with prohibition was large, these states were predominantly rural, low population states. By 1918, thirty-one states had adopted a prohibition law, but 52.1 percent of the population lived in wet states, and the distribution of states that passed prohibition laws before World War I was not random. Of the twenty-six that had prohibition laws, "fourteen were west of the Mississippi. Eight were south of the Ohio and Potomac. Two (Maine and New Hampshire) were in northern, rural New England" (Merz 1931: 19). Only two (Michigan and Indiana) were populated, industrial states.

The role of state prohibition is also not compelling because the laws in many states were weak; in particular, they fell far short of bone-dry prohibition (Merz 1931: 20–22). Many states allowed importation of certain quantities of alcohol and/or home manufacture. For example, Alabama allowed any citizen to import two quarts of distilled spirits or two gallons of wine or five gallons of beer every fifteen days.[6] And states had limited ability to enforce prohibitions given the openness of their borders.[7] Indeed, both wets and drys agreed the state laws were ineffective. Wets offered this as evidence prohibition was foolish, while drys used it to argue that only national prohibition could reduce alcohol consumption.

Figures 3.3 and 3.4 provide evidence on the possible effect of state prohibitions by showing data on cirrhosis for two groups of states: those that were wet throughout the pre-1920 period, and those that adopted prohibition at some point during this period. The figures present only a subset of the states in each category to avoid cluttering the graph; the statistical analysis in Dills and Miron (2003) considers the complete set of states.

The figures show that the most dramatic declines in cirrhosis occurred in states that were wet throughout the pre-1920 period, and these states included several of the most populous states (e.g.,

Figure 3.3

U.S. cirrhosis death rates in states without prohibition before 1919

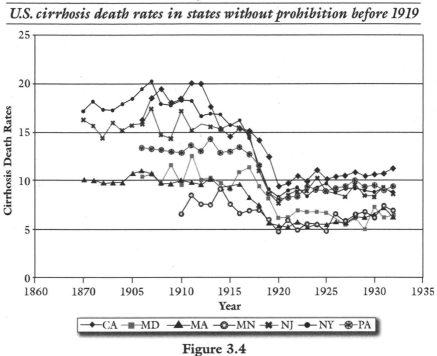

Figure 3.4

U.S. cirrhosis death rates in states adopting prohibition before 1919

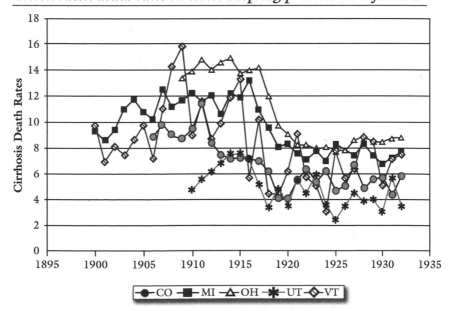

New York, Pennsylvania, New Jersey). There is some evidence of declines in states that adopted prohibition during this period, but the declines were smaller on average than the declines in wet states. These figures do not support the hypothesis that state prohibitions lowered cirrhosis death rates.

A further piece of evidence on state prohibitions comes from data on alcohol consumption and cirrhosis for the pre-1920 period, shown in Figure 3.5. The key fact is that cirrhosis declined first; indeed, alcohol consumption gives no indication of a decline until 1918, well after the wave of state prohibition adoptions. And the official data potentially overstate the 1918–1919 decline in alcohol consumption because federal laws passed during this period probably induced underreporting. For example, higher tax rates adopted in 1916–1917 might have encouraged home production, and the federal order to close the breweries and distilleries (see below) might have spawned illicit production. Thus, if one examines alcohol co-

Figure 3.5

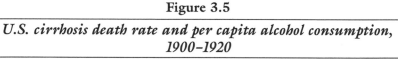

U.S. cirrhosis death rate and per capita alcohol consumption, 1900–1920

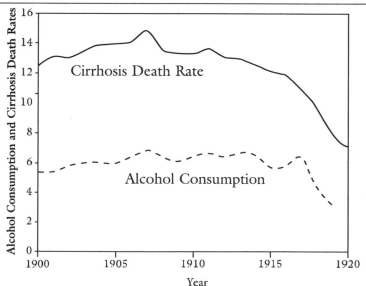

sumption, rather than cirrhosis, even the aggregate data suggest little effect of the state prohibitions.

An additional reason to question the role of state prohibitions is that adoption of alcohol prohibition is not an exogenous event, imposed on a state by forces outside its control. Instead, states choose whether to become dry, and this decision is plausibly related to the behavior of alcohol consumption within that state. States in which per capita alcohol consumption was relatively low might have been more likely to adopt dry laws. Similarly, states in which consumption was declining for other reasons (e.g., changing demographics) might also have faced less opposition to dry laws. To the extent adoption occurred in states where anti-alcohol sentiment was already increasing, comparisons of states with and without prohibition are biased toward finding a consumption-reducing effect even if none existed.

A second possible explanation for the pre-1920 decline in cirrhosis is federal regulation of alcohol. In February 1913, Congress adopted the Webb-Kenyon Law, which prohibited shipments of liquor from wet states into dry states if such shipments were in violation of the dry state law. This did not prohibit all shipments into dry states, since some allowed importation (Merz 1931: 14). In February 1917, Congress passed the Reed bone-dry amendment, which forbade interstate shipment of liquor into states that prohibited manufacture and sale, even if the state allowed importation (Merz 1931: 20). In August 1917, Congress adopted the Food Control Law, which forbade the manufacture of distilled spirits from any form of foodstuff and closed the distilleries; in September 1918, it closed the breweries as well (Merz 1931: 26–27, 40–41). Also in September 1918, Congress approved wartime prohibition, although this prohibition did not take effect until July 1, 1919 (Merz 1931: 41). The wartime prohibition act contained the first general restriction on sale, providing that after June 30, 1919, no liquor could be sold for beverage purposes except for export (Schmeckebier 1929: 4–5).

The timing of these federal restrictions on alcohol coincides roughly with the pre-1920 decline in cirrhosis, but several factors suggest these restrictions were unimportant in explaining the decline. These restrictions did not prevent consumption of imports or existing stocks, and the budget for enforcement was essentially zero. Further, most of these restrictions did not take effect until 1917 or later, while cirrhosis began declining as early as 1908 and had fallen substantially by 1917. And a number of other factors likely played a more direct role in the declines from 1917 to 1920, including a drastic reduction in immigration that took place during the earlier part of the decade, a major increase in alcohol tax rates that occurred in 1916–1917, World War I, and the worldwide flu epidemic of 1918, which killed tens of millions (Kolata 1999). These last two factors depleted the ranks of those susceptible of dying from cirrhosis, so the number of cirrhosis deaths was lower thereafter for some time (U.S. Bureau of the Census 1975: 58–62).

The facts presented so far weaken the impression that prohibition or pre-1920 anti-alcohol laws caused the low level of cirrhosis during the Prohibition period. A complete analysis, however, must account for a range of factors that potentially influence alcohol consumption, such as income, demographics, and alcohol tax rates. Dills and Miron (2003) present a detailed statistical analysis that accounts for these factors, concluding that national prohibition reduced cirrhosis by 10 to 20 percent.

This conclusion is surprising, since standard accounts suggest alcohol prices rose substantially during Prohibition, perhaps by several hundred percent on average (Warburton 1932; Fisher 1928). Thus, since available evidence suggests alcohol consumption is responsive to price (Leung and Phelps 1993), alcohol consumption should have declined dramatically.

One possible reconciliation is that the relevant price elasticity is in fact quite low. The proxy for alcohol consumption considered here, cirrhosis, is plausibly a better measure of heavy consumption than of moderate consumption. Theory does not suggest that heavy or addictive consumption is necessarily unresponsive to price (Becker and Murphy 1988), but evidence from micro data suggests heavy alcohol consumption is virtually price inelastic (Manning, Blumberg, and Moulton 1995).

A second possibility is that Prohibition created a forbidden fruit effect, thereby shifting preferences for alcohol and partially offsetting the depressing effect on demand of higher prices. This hypothesis receives anecdotal support in some contexts, and accounts of drinking behavior during Prohibition are consistent with such an effect (e.g., the term "roaring 20s"). Without more detailed evidence, however, one cannot interpret the results here as a strong indication of such an effect.

Still a third possibility is that the standard accounts of alcohol prices during Prohibition overstate the increase in price. Warburton's data compare prices between 1911–1915 and 1926–1930, while Fisher's compare prices between 1916 and 1928. Both authors examine the behavior of nominal prices, yet the price level increased by approximately 75 percent between these two periods (U.S. Bureau of the Census 1975: 211). Thus, at a minimum, the data presented by Warburton and Fisher overstate the increase in the relative price of alcohol.

In addition, Warburton presents a broad range of alcohol prices for the Prohibition period, and the lowest prices reported suggest that, even ignoring inflation, some alcoholic beverage prices fell relative to the pre-Prohibition period. This does not prove consumers paid less, on average, for alcohol, but they certainly faced an incentive to buy at the lowest prices and then stockpile the quantities purchased at these prices. The available data do not allow computation of the average price actually paid, and the high prices reported by Warburton in some cases allow for the possibility that the average price rose. But the magnitude of this rise is undoubtedly less than Fisher and Warburton asserted, and it is possible prices failed to rise substantially overall. If prices did not increase much, there is no puzzle in the modest decline in alcohol consumption.

Moreover, this possibility is consistent with the analysis in Chapter 2, which suggests the price-increasing effects of prohibition are not necessarily dramatic.

Implications for Drug Prohibition

The implications of this analysis for drug prohibition are significant. If drug prohibition also has modest effects on the price and consumption of drugs, then its key alleged benefit is moderate at best. And since other alleged benefits of prohibition, such as reduced crime, improved productivity, or better health, depend on the decrease in consumption, these benefits are likely modest as well.

Proponents of drug prohibition might respond that alcohol prohibition and current drug prohibition are not comparable, since the strictness of the law and the degree of enforcement have been greater under drug prohibition than under alcohol prohibition. Current drug prohibition does allow relatively few exceptions in comparison with alcohol prohibition, which permitted production of small quantities of alcohol for personal use, consumption of low alcohol wine and beer, and the use of alcohol in medicines and sacramental wines.[8] And the degree of drug prohibition enforcement during the last two decades has greatly exceeded anything that occurred under Prohibition. Nevertheless, the lessons of alcohol prohibition are relevant to current drug prohibition, for two reasons.

First, the analysis in Miron (2003a) suggests that despite the enormous level of resources devoted to enforcement, drug prohibition has not raised drug prices to nearly the degree suggested in most accounts. Previous analyses have suggested that prohibition makes drugs ten, twenty, or even hundreds of times more expensive than they would be if legal.[9] Much of this analysis, however, simply notes that the raw materials from which drugs are produced sell at "low" prices in producer countries while the finished products sell at "high" prices in consumer countries, implicitly attributing the entire "markup" to prohibition.

Such an analysis, however, does not account for the storage, transportation, distribution, and retailing costs that exist for any product, regardless of legal status, nor does this analysis recognize that black market suppliers generally evade various tax and regulatory costs incurred by legal suppliers. Thus, this approach does not say much about the effect of prohibition on prices. In fact, the farmgate-to-retail "markups" on many legal goods (such as coffee, chocolate, tea, or beer) are similar to or greater than the markups on cocaine and heroin; likewise, legal transactions in drugs (which are used for research, testing, and medical purposes) also suggest relatively modest effects of prohibition. Both sets of calculations imply that the black market price of cocaine is two to four times and the price of heroin six to nineteen times the legalized price.

A second reason to doubt that current drug prohibition has a substantially stronger effect on drug consumption than alcohol prohibition had on alcohol consumption is that over the past twenty years, enforcement of drug prohibition has increased substantially, but real, purity-adjusted drug prices have generally declined (Basov, Jacobson, and Miron 2001). For example, Caulkins and Reuter (1998) show the real price of cocaine falling from over $450 per pure gram in 1981 to roughly $100 per pure gram in 1996. DiNardo (1993) finds no evidence that enforcement, as measured by cocaine seizures, raised cocaine prices or reduced cocaine use among high school seniors during the 1980s. Yuan and Caulkins (1998) find that a greater number of drug seizures is associated with lower black market prices of cocaine and heroin. Basov, Jacobson, and Miron (2001) show that despite the enormous increase in prohibition enforcement that has occurred over the past twenty-five years, drug use appears little different now than at the beginning of the escalation in enforcement. Kuziemko and Levitt (2003) suggest that increases in enforcement since 1985 have reduced cocaine consumption by 10–15 percent; since enforcement has increased substantially over this period, this again suggests that prohibition has a moderate but not a dramatic effect in reducing drug consumption. There is thus little evidence that enforcement under current drug prohibition has raised drug prices or decreased drug consumption to a substantial degree.

More generally, several kinds of evidence fail to indicate a substantial impact of drug prohibition on drug consumption. Figure 3.6 presents data on the per capita consumption of opiates for the years prior to 1914, the year in which the Harrison Narcotics Act first criminalized opiates, cocaine, and other drugs. The figure shows that per capita consumption increased on average until the mid-1890s and then decreased steadily until 1914.[10] The existence of such substantial fluctuations in the absence of prohibition suggests many factors affect opiate consumption, not just government policy. These factors include demographics, per capita income, wars, and the like. In particular, public health concerns raised by the medical profession appear to have been the major reason for the substantial decline in opiate use between the mid-1890s and 1914 (Musto 1973: 1–6).

Figure 3.6

Pounds of opium entered for consumption annually 1855–1926, per capita

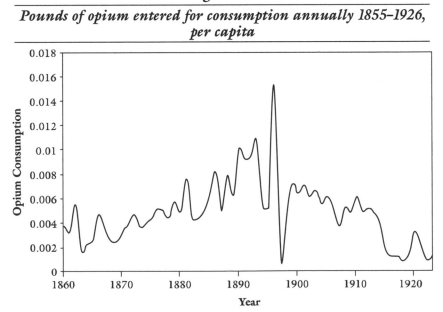

A different kind of evidence comes from the experience of U.S. states that decriminalized marijuana at various points during the 1970s. Under decriminalization, the penalties for possession of small amounts of marijuana (typically one ounce or less) are changed from felonies, punishable by jail terms and heavy fines, to misdemeanors, punishable by small fines only. The evidence provided by decriminalization is potentially weak; changes in the law sometimes ratify *ex post* what has already taken place, and the fact that some states change their laws while others do not might reflect incidental factors rather than any real difference in enforcement. Thus, it is possible enforcement of marijuana laws did not change much in decriminalizing states or changed across states in ways that do not bear a close relation to the criminal status of marijuana (Pacula, Chriqui, and King 2003). Nevertheless, existing evidence provides little indication that marijuana decriminalization was accompanied by increased marijuana use.[11]

One additional piece of evidence comes from comparing drug use rates between the United States and other rich countries such as those in Western Europe, Japan, or Australia.[12] These other countries have prohibition laws similar in broad structure to those in the United States, especially for harder drugs such as cocaine and heroin. The degree to which these countries enforce their prohibition regimes, however, is markedly less (Miron 2001b). Thus, if prohibition is an effective method of reducing drug use, these countries should have use rates noticeably higher than in the United States. As shown in Table 3.2, however, there is no evidence these countries have higher drug use rates; indeed the U.S. rate frequently exceeds that in most other countries. This evidence is only suggestive, since it does not control for other factors. But it fails to provide evidence that prohibition reduces drug use.

A final issue that arises in interpreting the results here concerns what constitutes a "large" effect of prohibition. If one credits Prohibition for the entire fall in cirrhosis from, say, 1915 to 1925, this suggests Prohibition reduced alcohol consumption by roughly

Table 3.2

*Percentage of population age 15 and over using illicit drugs,
late 1990s–2003*

	Opiates	Cocaine	Cannabis
United States	0.6	2.6	9.3
Austria	0.3	0.6	5.0
Belgium	0.4	0.8	6.1
Denmark	0.4	0.5	4.4
Finland	0.1	0.2	2.2
France	0.4	0.2	8.4
Germany	0.3	0.9	6.0
Greece	0.5	0.9	4.4
Ireland	0.4	1.3	9.4
Italy	0.8	0.8	6.2
Liechtenstein	0.03	0.08	0.5
Luxembourg	0.9	0.4	4.0
Malta	0.3	0.03	0.8
Monaco	0.1	0.01	0.4
Netherlands	0.3	1.2	5.6
Norway	0.4	0.6	4.5
Portugal	0.9	0.3	3.3
San Marino	0.02	0.04	4.0
Spain	0.6	2.6	9.9
Sweden	0.08	.05	1.0
Switzerland	0.5	0.4	7.0
United Kingdom	0.6	2.0	10.6
Australia	0.6	1.5	15.0
New Zealand	0.7	0.5	13.4
Japan	0.02		0.05

Source: Global Illicit Drug Trends 2003 (339–351),
ODCCP Studies on Drugs and Crime, New York: United National Office
for Drug Control and Crime Prevention, 2003. Available on-line at:
http://www.undcp.org/global_illicit_drug_trends.html, accessed 12/13/03.

50 percent. This is a substantial decline by many standards, but it is nevertheless modest in comparison to assertions about the effect of legalization on drug use. These assertions (e.g., Levitt 2003) claim that drug use would mushroom, creating a several-fold increase in the number of "addicts." The evidence from alcohol prohibition does not support such assertions. Whether the "benefit" of a 50 percent reduction in drug or alcohol consumption is worth the negative consequences detailed above, and whether these can be achieved via other methods, are issues discussed later. But the right question is how these costs compare to moderate increases in consumption, not to the outlandish figures frequently bandied about by supporters of current prohibition.

Notes

1. An additional difficulty is that a given country's policy might reflect its attitudes toward drugs. For example, populations that are more tolerant of drug use might be less likely to adopt or enforce prohibition. In this case, drug use would be higher in places with less restrictive regimes, but the higher rate would not necessarily be due to the absence of prohibition.

2. See, in particular, Warburton (1932), as well as other references cited below.

3. A few analyses of prohibition have considered additional indicators. For example, Miron and Zwiebel (1991) find that deaths from alcoholism, admittances to mental hospitals for alcohol psychosis, and arrests for drunkenness follow roughly the same pattern as the cirrhosis death rate. See also Warburton (1932).

4. Dills and Miron (2003) examine the relation between cirrhosis and alcohol consumption using data for sixteen countries. They document that cirrhosis is positively correlated with alcohol consumption in most cases, but the relationship is far from perfect.

5. See, for example, Aaron and Musto (1981); Moore and Gerstein (1981), Edwards et al. (1994); Musto (1996); MacCoun and Reuter (2001); and Yoon et. al (2001).

6. Similarly, Virginia law allowed importation of one quart of distilled spirits or three gallons of beer or one gallon of wine every thirty days, except for students at a university, college, or other school; minors; or a female

not the head of household. Indiana law stated that it did not intend to interfere with domestic manufacture of wine. Michigan, New Hampshire, Iowa, and North Dakota laws did not prohibit importation for personal use. Mississippi law permitted manufacture of homemade wine. North Carolina allowed importation of one quart of spirits or five gallons of beer every fifteen days. West Virginia permitted manufacture of wine for personal use and importation of one quart of liquor every thirty days. Tennessee permitted manufacture for personal use. South Carolina allowed importation of one quart of liquor every thirty days for medicinal purposes (Merz 1931: 20–22).

7. Isaac (1965) provides a detailed analysis of the prohibition movement in Tennessee up to the passage of constitutional prohibition. He describes both the legal regime and enforcement as weak during the first few years of state prohibition, 1909–1913, and he suggests that alcohol consumption continued without much interruption in the larger cities. He also describes the legal regime and the degree of enforcement as becoming gradually stricter beginning in 1914, but he suggests that liquor was still widely available, at least in the major cities.

8. Some medicinal and religious uses of prohibited drugs are legal under current drug prohibition, but the range of circumstances is narrow.

9. See, for example, Friedman (1972); Reuter and Kleiman (1986); Moore (1990); Nadelmann (1991); Morgan (1991); Koper and Reuter (1996); Caulkins and Reuter (1998); Levitt (2003).

10. The Harrison Act did not prohibit marijuana; this resulted from the 1937 Marijuana Tax Act. Data on opium are also available after 1914 because importation of opium for medical purposes continued. A black market arose soon after 1914, however, so these data are not reliable indicators of consumption (Terry and Pellens 1928: 49). The spike in opium "consumption" in 1897 reflects importation in advance of an announced tariff on opium (Terry and Pellens 1928: 745–746).

11. Miron (2002) provides a review of this evidence.

12. I limit the comparison to such countries because it controls at least partially for other possible determinants of drug use and because the data for such countries are more likely comparable to those for the United States.

4

Prohibitions and Violence

The second critical issue in the analysis of drug prohibition is its effect on crime, especially violence. As noted earlier, the standard defense of prohibition asserts that drug consumption encourages violence and that by reducing drug use, prohibition reduces violence. The evidence reviewed in Chapter 3 suggests that prohibition's impact on drug consumption is modest, which implies any violence-reducing effect of prohibition is also modest. In addition, the discussion in Chapter 2 shows prohibition might encourage the violent resolution of commercial disputes and thereby increase violence, even if it substantially reduces drug use. And the discussion there makes clear that little evidence suggests a causal effect of drug use on violence. Nevertheless, the question of whether prohibition decreases or increases violence is an empirical one.

This chapter first examines the relation between homicide and the enforcement of alcohol and drug prohibition over the past century in the United States. It then considers the relation between homicide rates and prohibition enforcement across countries. In both cases, the evidence provides no indication that prohibition reduces violence; in fact, enforcement is consistently associated with higher rates of violence.[1]

The Effect of Prohibition and the Effect of Enforcement

As a first step in analyzing the effect of prohibition on violence, it is necessary to distinguish between prohibition per se and the enforcement of prohibition by means of arrests, fines, prison terms, and other sanctions. The simplest hypothesis about the relation between prohibition and violence is that prohibiting a good or activity forces the market underground and thereby encourages market participants to use violence in the resolution of disputes. This hypothesis is a good starting point, but numerous examples suggest it is incomplete. In particular, many prohibitions are not associated with elevated violence rates, and even for those that are, violence changes substantially during a given prohibition regime.

The factor that determines how much a given prohibition induces violence is the level of enforcement. Prohibitions are unlikely to create violence unless there is substantial enforcement, and the amount of violence increases with the degree of enforcement. There are two main reasons.

First, prohibitions rarely create black markets unless there is a substantial degree of enforcement, and the size of the black market normally increases with the degree of enforcement. The reason is that prohibition is not a total ban on the production, sale, and possession of drugs; rather, prohibition contains numerous exceptions, such as medical, research, and scientific uses of drugs. These exceptions permit legal or quasi-legal production and consumption of drugs, thus allowing use of standard, nonviolent mechanisms to resolve disagreements related to the drug trade. Increased enforcement, however, in the form of laws that decrease the scope of the exceptions, or increased monitoring of existing exceptions, places some additional transactions outside the realm of legal dispute resolution mechanisms.

There are many examples of the legal provision of "illegal" drugs within a prohibition regime. The United States did not treat the maintenance of opiate users by physicians as proscribed until several years after prohibition took effect (Musto 1973). Similarly, England allowed doctors relatively free reign in dispensing heroin for the first several decades of its drug prohibition, although since the 1960s it has imposed greater limits on heroin maintenance. Under current prohibition in the United States, doctors can prescribe many otherwise prohibited drugs, such as morphine and codeine, and many countries operate treatment programs that provide methadone or heroin to certain drug users. Similarly, it was legal during Prohibition to produce small quantities of alcohol for personal use, to produce certain kinds of low alcohol wine and beer, to put alcohol in medicines and sacramental wines, and to use alcohol in industrial products.[2]

The critical aspect of all these examples is that, when exceptions to prohibition exist, at least some manufacturing, transportation, and distribution of drugs is legal; thus, this component of the drug trade is unlikely to generate violence. If the exceptions to the prohibition are broad, or if the restrictions are weakly enforced, then the exceptions permit a substantial component of the market to remain above ground, reducing the incentives for violence.

The second reason enforcement is critical to the degree of violence generated by prohibition is that enforcement prevents black market participants from utilizing mechanisms that avoid violence. For example, the arrest of one supplier from a cartel generates violence among the remaining suppliers as they attempt to capture the arrested supplier's market share. Alternatively, enforcement that creates turnover among suppliers makes it difficult to establish a reputation for swift and violent retaliation, which implies greater violence on average. Likewise, enforcement that generates turnover among suppliers makes it hard for consumers to purchase repeatedly from a reliable supplier, increasing the scope for disagreements. High levels of enforcement also discourage production and distribution methods that minimize transactions, such as home production of marijuana.

Beyond the two effects of increased enforcement discussed earlier—increasing the black market's share of the drug market, and increasing the likelihood of violence for a given-size black market—there are several other mechanisms by which increased enforcement might increase the level of violence under prohibition.

As noted previously, increased enforcement of prohibition for a given-size criminal justice budget implies reduced enforcement of laws against homicide, robbery, assault, and the like. This arises, for example, when prisons release violent offenders early to make room for drug offenders. Similarly, the resources devoted to prohibition enforcement can "crowd out" enforcement of property rights in other sectors, thus encouraging participants to employ violence (e.g., Russia after the fall of communism). And the resources devoted to drug enforcement are unavailable for fighting guerrilla groups, such as the FARC in Colombia or the Shining Path in Peru, which generate violence for independent reasons.

A different way prohibition encourages violence is by making consumers or producers of the prohibited commodity less likely to use the official dispute resolution system for disputes not related to the prohibited commodity. For example, a drug user or seller who has been robbed of non-drug items might not report this to the police—since this could risk sanctions related to possession or sale of drugs—and instead sanction the robber himself, possibly using violence. And higher enforcement increases this effect. If police routinely overlook small quantities of drugs, the effect is small; if police routinely hassle anyone thought to be associated with drugs, the effect is large.

Evidence on Violence and Drug and Alcohol Prohibition

A first piece of evidence on the relation between enforcement and violence comes from the behavior of the homicide rate over the past century in the United States. Homicide is not the only kind of violence potentially fostered by prohibition, but homicide data are available for a longer time span than are other measures of violence, which permits analysis of alcohol prohibition as well as drug prohibition. Moreover, vital statistics data such as those available on homicide are generally superior to crime statistics such as those available on assault, robbery, or rape.

Figure 4.1 presents data on the homicide rate in the United States for the period 1900–1995.[3] Beginning around 1910, the homicide rate rises steadily through 1933, when it begins a general decline until approximately 1960, interrupted by a spike during World War II. Beginning in the early 1960s, the homicide rate rises steadily until the mid-1970s—to a level slightly above the previous peak in 1933—and then fluctuates around a relatively high value for the remainder of the sample.

Figure 4.1

U.S. homicide rate (per 100,000)

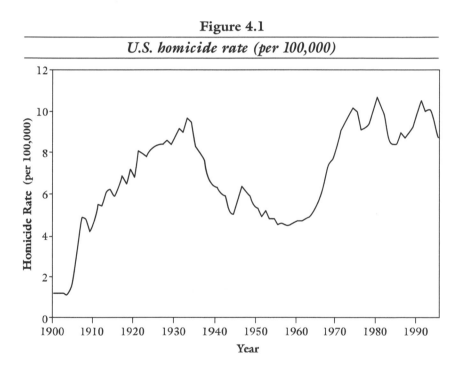

These data are instructive in several ways. Roughly speaking there have been two periods with high homicide rates in U.S. history, the 1920–1933 period and the 1970–1990 period. Both before the first episode and between these two episodes, the homicide rate was relatively low or clearly declining. This pattern appears inconsistent with a number of hypotheses about the causes of violence. For example, restrictions on handguns and other weapons have been more extensive in the 1965–1995 period than during the 1945–1965 period, yet homicide rates have consistently been higher during the period with greater controls. Urbanization has proceeded, if not at a steady rate, at least always in an upward direction over this sample, yet violence rates have gone up and come down dramatically. The incarceration rate, a crude measure of the overall degree of criminal justice deterrence, fluctuated within a narrow range from about 1930 to 1970, during which time the homicide rate both declined substantially and rose substantially; the incarceration rate then increased by a factor of more than four between 1970 and 1995, during which time the homicide rate exhibited several significant ups and downs. And use of the death penalty fell substantially from the mid-1930s to the mid-1960s, precisely the period over which the homicide rate declined markedly as well. None of this demonstrates that these variables play no role in explaining the homicide rate, but the absence of a correlation fails to make a prima facie case in that direction.

By contrast, the hypothesis that drug prohibition and alcohol prohibition cause violence is broadly consistent with these data (Friedman 1991). The homicide rate was high in the 1920–1933 period, when constitutional prohibition of alcohol was in effect, and in the 1970–1990 period, when drug prohibition was enforced to a relatively stringent degree. After repeal of alcohol prohibition, the homicide rate dropped quickly and remained low during a period when drug prohibition, although in existence, was not vigorously enforced. And the homicide rate was lowest at the beginning of the sample, when neither alcohol nor drug prohibition existed at the federal level and only in a minor way at the state level.

Despite this prima facie consistency, however, there are challenges for the prohibition-causes-violence hypothesis. The homicide rate began increasing as early as 1906, and increases to some degree throughout the next decade, even though constitutional prohibition of alcohol did not take effect until 1920.[4] And the homicide rate fluctuated substantially after 1937, even without any change in alcohol prohibition (which was repealed in 1933) or drug prohibition (which was in effect continuously through this period).

The critical omitted factor in the relation between prohibition and violence is the degree of prohibition enforcement. To see this, consider Figure 4.2, which plots a measure of drug and alcohol prohibition enforcement over the past century. The measure presented is the real, per capita, federal expenditure for enforcement of alcohol and drug prohibition by the agency or agencies devoted solely to that mission.[5] The figure suggests a strong, positive relation between enforcement of prohibition and the homicide rate. Enforcement climbs along with the homicide rate during Prohibition and then falls at the end of the period, as does the homicide rate. Enforcement is relatively low during the 1940s and 1950s, as is the homicide rate for the most part. And enforcement of prohibition rises along with the homicide rate beginning after 1960.

Figure 4.2

Expenditure for enforcement of alcohol and drug prohibition (dollars per capita)

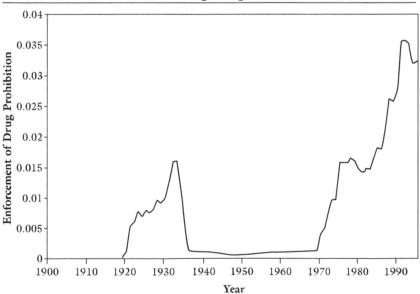

Other possible measures of enforcement that are available for shorter time spans (e.g., arrests, asset seizures, drug seizures and the like) tell a story similar to that implied by Figures 4.1 and 4.2.

The strong correlation between enforcement and homicide makes a suggestive case that enforcement of drug and alcohol prohibition raises the homicide rate, but the correlation might reflect other factors that influence homicide and correlate with enforcement. To address this issue, Miron (1999) examines the impact of enforcement on homicide, controlling for factors such as the age composition of the population, the incarceration rate, the use of the death penalty, per capita income, the unemployment rate, support for marijuana legalization, or gun ownership. This more detailed statistical analysis shows consistently that higher enforcement is associated with higher homicide, even controlling for other factors.[6]

The critical caveat that arises in interpreting these results is that a society experiencing increased violence might increase its enforcement of drug or alcohol prohibition, implying enforcement depends on the level of violence. In this case violence and enforcement can be positively correlated even if enforcement reduces or does not affect violence, and a positive correlation between enforcement and violence would not necessarily indicate that enforcement per se produces violence.

The possibility of "reverse causation" cannot be dismissed on a priori grounds, but it appears unlikely to be the main reason for the correlation between homicide and enforcement. The correlation persists across both the alcohol prohibition and the drug prohibition subsamples, even though a number of factors might have changed the feedback mechanism from violence to enforcement between these two periods (e.g., the speed with which data on crime become available). Likewise, the correlation is not much affected by omitting the 1980s and 1990s, the period during which the crack epidemic created enormous concern about drugs and violence.

Setting aside this caveat, the estimated impact of enforcement on homicide is not only positive but large; it suggests that eliminating drug prohibition would reduce homicide in the United States by 25–75 percent. Interestingly, this estimate suggests a fraction of all homicides due to disputes arising in the illegal drug trade that is consistent with cross-sectional, individual level data. Goldstein et al. (1989), using police reports and police evaluations, examine the causes of all homicides in a sample of New York City precincts during part of the year 1988. They determine that more than half of the homicides were due to drug-related factors, but almost three quarters reflected "systemic" factors (Goldstein 1985), meaning disputes over drug territory, drug debts, and other drug-trade related issues. Thus, approximately 39 percent of the homicides resulted from the inability of drug market participants to settle disputes using the official dispute resolution system.

Violence and Drug Prohibition Across Countries

The analysis so far has suggested that enforcement of alcohol and drug prohibition in the United States caused the main fluctuations in homicide rates over the past hundred years. There are reasons to interpret these results cautiously, but at a minimum they fail to suggest that prohibition reduces violence.

A different piece of evidence on the relation between prohibition enforcement and violence comes from comparisons of violence across countries that enforce prohibition to varying degrees. Violence rates differ dramatically across countries. This is a puzzle for the view that prohibition per se causes violence, since virtually all countries have drug prohibition regimes similar to that in the United States.[7] The degree of enforcement differs substantially, however, so the mechanisms described above potentially explain why Europe has a much lower violence rate than the United States. Conventional wisdom holds, in particular, that European countries rely far less on criminal sanctions than the United States, preferring

Table 4.1

Homicide rates, 1993–1996 (per 100,000)

United States	9.30	Argentina	4.40
Austria	1.17	Chile	2.75
Canada	1.73	Colombia	83.50
Denmark	1.21	Ecuador	12.63
Finland	3.13	Guyana	4.60
France	1.10	Paraguay	9.80
Germany	1.15	Venezuela	15.30
Greece	1.33	Azerbaijan	29.85
Iceland	0.13	Belarus	10.40
Ireland	0.65	Bulgaria	5.00
Italy	1.70	Croatia	4.05
Luxembourg	0.80	Czech Republic	2.10
Malta	1.20	Estonia	24.03
Netherlands	1.20	Hungary	3.70
Norway	0.93	Kazakhstan	18.43
Portugal	1.50	Kyrgyzstan	12.35
Spain	0.93	Latvia	21.97
Sweden	1.18	Lithuania	11.73
Switzerland	1.32	Moldova	14.50
U.K.	1.00	Poland	2.78
Australia	1.73	Romania	4.15
New Zealand	1.75	Russia	29.98
Hong Kong	1.23	Slovakia	2.40
Japan	0.60	Slovenia	1.98
Korea	1.60	Turkmenistan	4.50
Singapore	1.55	Ukraine	15.00
Bahamas	16.17	Uzbekistan	4.30
Barbados	7.33	China	1.13
Costa Rica	5.55	Israel	1.73
Cuba	7.83	Kuwait	1.60
Mexico	17.27	Macau	3.20
Nicaragua	5.30	Mauritius	2.10
Trinidad/Tobago	10.75	Philippines	11.50

Source: Miron (2001)

medical or public health approaches.[8] Given this fact, the elevated rate of violence in the United States plausibly results from greater drug prohibition enforcement.[9]

To assess the validity of this hypothesis, Table 4.1 presents vital statistics data on homicide rates in sixty-six countries. The set of countries consists of all those for which data are available in at least one of the years 1993–1996, and the figures in the table are the average rates over this period.

The data show first that homicide rates differ substantially across countries. The U.S. homicide rate averages approximately 9 per 100,000 during the sample period, which is five to nine times the rate in most Western-style democracies. At the same time, the U.S. homicide rate is similar to or less than the rate in many countries. Seven Central or South American countries have homicide rates in excess of the U.S. rate, and several others have rates that are close. Every country in this group has a homicide rate in excess of the average for the rich countries other than the United States. Similarly, ten of the twenty former Soviet Bloc countries have rates that exceed the U.S. rate, with practically every country in this group having a homicide rate in excess of the non-U.S., rich country average. Thus, the level of homicide in the United States stands out in comparison to other rich, democratic countries, but not in comparison to the world as a whole.

These data are partially, but not entirely, suggestive of the main hypothesis considered here. On the one hand, violence rates are high in the countries of the Caribbean and Latin America, most of which are key producers of, or transit points for, illegal drugs. Colombia's homicide rate, in particular, is roughly ten times the U.S. rate. The fact that these countries produce and ship illegal drugs does not necessarily mean they should be violent, given the framework outlined previously; the hypothesis here is that the degree of enforcement plays a crucial role. But the existence of a substantial black market is necessary for enforcement to encourage violence.

On the other hand, violence rates are also high in the countries of the former Soviet Bloc, which are less obviously important producers or transporters of illegal drugs. This does not mean prohibition enforcement plays no role in these elevated violence rates; these countries consume illegal drugs, and they have illegal drug markets that are potentially violent. But much of their violence might reflect ethnic conflict or the lack of an effective criminal justice system, rather than prohibition enforcement. If the violence is due to either of these two mechanisms, however, it is still consistent with the broader perspective proposed here, which is that violence is high when alternative dispute resolution mechanisms are not readily available.

To examine formally the hypothesis that differences in drug prohibition enforcement explain differences in violence, Miron (2001b) presents a more detailed statistical analysis that utilizes drug seizures by law enforcement authorities as a measure of enforcement and accounts for differences across countries in gun control laws, income per capita, the percentage of the population that is male aged 15–24, the percentage of the population in urban areas, population density, educational attainment, and use of the death penalty.[10] The empirical results consistently support the hypotheses that prohibition enforcement increases violence.

As with the time-series analysis of U.S. data discussed above, the positive correlation between enforcement and homicide is not decisive evidence that prohibition *causes* violence because causation might flow in the other direction. Drug seizures might be high in some countries because use rates are high, in which case the positive correlation is consistent with an effect of drug use on violence.[11] Alternatively, assuming seizure rates reflect enforcement differences, the positive correlation with violence might occur because countries with elevated violence choose strict enforcement of drug prohibition.

Again, this possibility cannot be ruled out a priori, but several considerations suggest reverse causation is a small part of the story.

As noted earlier, there is little convincing evidence that drug use has an independent effect in precipitating violence. Moreover, existing data on drug use across countries (United Nations Office on Drugs and Crime 2003) show, if anything, a negative correlation between drug use and homicide. And the differences in drug prohibition enforcement across countries plausibly reflect several factors other than the level of violence. For example, the strong enforcement in Latin America results in part from U.S. attempts to address its own drug or crime problems, not from events in Latin America. Thus, the differences in prohibition enforcement are mainly predetermined relative to homicide over the time horizons considered here, in which case a causal interpretation of the results is reasonable.

Discussion

The results above indicate that comparisons over time within the United States, and comparisons across countries in recent years, both demonstrate the same pattern: high rates of prohibition enforcement are associated with high rates of violence. Results for alcohol prohibition are also consistent with this conclusion, as are analyses that use data across or within cities, counties, and countries.[12]

This robust positive relation between prohibition enforcement and violence could partly reflect policy endogeneity, as noted previously, so the exact degree to which prohibition induces violence is difficult to pin down. But the standard defense of prohibition assumes enforcement *reduces* violence, in stark contrast to these results. Thus, whatever its limitations, the evidence provides no support for prohibition.

Notes

1. The analysis is based on Miron (1999, 2001b).
2. The alcohol used for industrial purposes differs chemically from beverage alcohol and is in fact poisonous. It can be converted to beverage alcohol with little difficulty, however.

3. The numbers at the beginning of the sample are sufficiently unusual to raise questions of data comparability; the changes in the homicide rate from 1.3 in 1904 to 2.1 in 1905 to 3.9 in 1906 are large in comparison to virtually all subsequent fluctuations. One plausible explanation is that the states reporting data on homicides accounted for only 26 percent of the population in 1900, but 50 percent in 1910, 80 percent in 1920, and 100 percent in 1933 (U.S. Bureau of the Census 1975: 408). Moreover, the states in the initial sample had relatively low homicide rates (Eckberg 1995). Thus, especially for the first decade of the century, data from additional states might have raised the overall homicide rate simply because of differences across states. By 1910, this problem is necessarily diminishing in importance, so there is a case for excluding, say, the first ten years of data from the analysis. As shown in Miron (1999), however, the key empirical results are generally strengthened by omission of these potentially problematic observations. Also, the use of Eckberg's (1995) "corrected" homicide rate series provides results that are similar—if anything, stronger—than those presented here.

4. This statement refers to the official, Vital Statistics series on homicides presented in Figure 4.1. There is less of an anomaly in the alternate series offered by Eckberg (1995), which does not display such large increases during the first two decades of the century.

5. For most of the period, this is simply the budget of the Drug Enforcement Administration (DEA) and its predecessors; in a few years, it combines the budget of the DEA and similar agencies. See Miron (1999) for details.

6. The statistical analysis presented in Miron (1999) also addresses the possibility of lags in the relation between enforcement and homicide; this has little effect on the results.

7. In recent years, a number of European countries have weakened their prohibition laws substantially; see http://eldd.emcdda.eu.int and http://www.norml.org for details.

8. See, e.g., Gordon 1991; Bull, McDowell, Norberry, Strang, and Wardlaw 1992; Reuter, Falco, and MacCoun 1993.

9. Moreover, the fact that drug prohibition is lax in certain countries, implying low rates of violence, potentially explains why the restrictive gun laws in countries like England or Japan have not themselves given rise to violent black markets in guns: the low rate of drug prohibition-induced violence implies a minimal demand for guns and thus small or nonexistent black markets for guns. This reasoning also suggests why comparing violence rates with gun ownership rates might confuse the direction of causation; gun ownership rates might be high because violence is high, which in turn reflects drug prohibition.

10. That analysis also finds that stricter gun control laws are associated with higher homicide rates. This might reflect the fact that gun prohibition creates violence, via the mechanisms described above. Alternatively, it might indicate that violent countries are prone to adopt restrictive gun control laws.

11. A different limitation of the seizure rate is that it takes no account of differences in drug treatment and drug maintenance. In practice, inclusion of such information might strengthen the results, since several European countries with high seizure rates (e.g., the Netherlands) also have generous treatment or maintenance policies.

12. The work by Goldstein et al. (1989) cited earlier, based on individual-level homicide data for New York City, finds that a substantial fraction of homicides reflect disputes over drug territory, drug debts, and other drug-trade related issues. Brumm and Cloninger (1995) find that higher drug prohibition arrest rates are associated with higher homicide offense rates across a sample of U.S. cities, while Resignato (2000) finds the same result within U.S. cities over time. Rasmussen, Benson, and Sollars (1993) find that a higher drug arrest rate is positively associated with the violent crime rate in a cross-section of Florida jurisdictions in 1989. Fajnzylber, Lederman, and Loayza (1998, 1999) find for the period 1970–1994 that being a drug-producing country or having a high drug-possession arrest rate is positively associated with a higher homicide rate. Shephard and Blackley (2003) find for the 1996–2000 period that drug arrest rates are generally positively associated with crime rates over time within counties in New York State. Thus, a broad range of evidence is consistent with the hypothesis that prohibition increases violence.

5

Is Prohibition Good Policy?

The preceding discussion has provided a theoretical framework in which to analyze the effects of prohibition, and it has discussed evidence on the degree to which prohibition reduces drug consumption and increases violence. All the analysis so far has been what economists call a positive analysis, meaning one that examines the consequences of a particular policy without addressing whether that policy is good or bad overall.

I now present a normative analysis of drug prohibition, meaning one that asks whether prohibition is preferable to legalization. The starting point is the observation that most effects of prohibition, such as increased violence and corruption, are unambiguously negative. The key issue, therefore, is prohibition's impact on drug consumption.

This chapter discusses four different perspectives on how public policy should treat drug consumption. In so doing, it emphasizes the distinction between two questions: whether policy should attempt to reduce such consumption; and whether prohibition is the right policy for achieving this objective, if the objective is sensible in the first place.[1]

Rational Consumption

One view of drug consumption—the one assumed in the standard economic paradigm—is that people consume drugs because they think such consumption makes them better off. According to this view, it does not matter whether people consume drugs because they like the psychopharmacological effects, because they believe drugs have medicinal properties, or because they think drugs are cool; all that matters is that they voluntarily choose to consume drugs. Similarly, under this view, it does not matter whether drugs are addictive or if consumption adversely affects health or productivity; if rational people choose to accept these risks, they must think the benefits are worth the costs.

The rational model of consumption was long believed to be inconsistent with many observed behaviors related to drug consumption, such as addiction, withdrawal, relapse, and the like. Theoretical work by Becker and Murphy (1988) shows that the rational model is potentially consistent with these phenomena, and a body of empirical work has had some success in fitting the model to data.[2] This does not mean the rational model is an accurate description of all drug consumption, but it undermines the presumption that all drug use (or other addictive consumption) is necessarily irrational.[3]

If one assumes the rational model describes most drug consumption, then the normative analysis of policies to reduce drug consumption is simple: any policy-induced reduction in drug use is a cost rather than a benefit. The reason is that, according to this model, consumers rationally choose drug consumption, so policy-induced reductions make them worse off. Thus, even a policy that has no undesirable side effects reduces welfare; in particular, such a policy harms drug users without benefiting anyone else.

The normative analysis of policy cannot stop at this point because the rational model of drug consumption strikes many observers as inaccurate. No doubt there are some individuals for whom this description is not appropriate.

It is self-evident, however, that many drug users are rational. Millions of people enjoy the high associated with marijuana; others value the pain relief or mental calm produced by opiates; still others appreciate the stimulation of cocaine. In this respect, consumption of prohibited drugs is no different from consumption of alcohol, gambling, or fatty foods. In each case, large numbers of persons enjoy these goods and integrate their consumption with normal, productive lives even though a minority find themselves challenged with problems of self-control.[4]

Objective evaluations should recognize, therefore, that the appropriate goal for policy is not elimination of all drug consumption, just as the goal of current policy is not elimination of all alcohol consumption. If some drug use does not fit the rational model, there is potentially a case (subject to caveats discussed later) for reducing consumption that is not rational. But the ideal policy reduces non-rational consumption without reducing rational consumption. Just as importantly, any reduction in rational drug consumption is a cost of policies that try to reduce non-rational drug consumption.

Externalities

A second perspective on drug consumption holds that such consumption can harm innocent third parties and thus be excessive from society's perspective, even if this consumption is individually rational. The standard economics term for such effects is negative externalities. For example, drug consumption can impair one's ability to drive a car or operate heavy machinery; it can adversely affect the health of the fetus; or it can cause additional use of publicly funded health care. And if drug use lowers productivity and therefore decreases earnings, there is a negative externality because drug users pay less in taxes, thereby imposing a greater burden on others for a given level of government expenditure.

There is no question drug consumption generates externalities in some cases. Most accounts greatly exaggerate the extent of these externalities, however; nor are these externalities obviously different from those of other, legal goods.

One commonly discussed externality from drug consumption is automobile accidents that occur if drug users drive under the influence. Such incidents are indeed an externality and a legitimate object of public policy concern. But the magnitude of this externality is not obviously large, and several controlled studies conclude that marijuana has a smaller detrimental effect on driving performance than alcohol.[5]

A different possible externality is harm to the unborn fetus caused by drug use during pregnancy. There is little debate that negative effects can occur, but these have not been adequately documented, the existing evidence is mixed, and this evidence suffers severe methodological problems in any case.[6] Many studies that document a correlation between drug use and negative pregnancy outcomes control imperfectly for other relevant factors such as use of alcohol and tobacco, access to prenatal care, income, presence of a father, or nutrition. Moreover, these studies do not control for unmeasured characteristics that plausibly correlate with drug use and also affect pregnancy outcomes (e.g., concern for the fetus). In addition, any negative effects of drug use are not obviously different from those of legal goods such as alcohol or cigarettes.

A different possible externality from drug use is workplace accidents; those involving the transportation industry have received particular attention. The evidence that illicit drugs play an important role in causing such accidents is at best mixed, and alcohol is implicated at least as often as illicit drugs (National Research Council 1994: 144–152). Kaestner and Grossman (1998) examine the relationship between drug use and workplace accidents. For males they find weak evidence that drug users have a higher accident rate than non-users; for females, they find no evidence of such an effect. Their evidence shows only whether drug users have elevated accident rates; it does not show that drug use caused these accidents.

In addition to being far less important than commonly believed, the externality-causing potential of drug consumption does not distinguish it from a broad array of other goods. As noted, the consumption of alcohol can impair driving ability or cause industrial accidents. The consumption of tobacco or saturated fat can increase the likelihood of using publicly funded health care. Driving on public roads exacerbates congestion and increases the travel time of others. Staying up late to watch television causes fatigue, thereby diminishing productivity or increasing the chance of accidents. Over-the-counter medications such as antihistamines cause drowsiness, which increases the likelihood of accidents. Saving too little for retirement places a burden on others by increasing eligibility for old-age medical or income insurance. And these are but a few examples.

The existing evidence thus suggests the externalities from drug consumption are far smaller than typically suggested and not obviously different from those of many legal goods. Further, calculating the net externalities from drug consumption is potentially tricky. For example, the net effect of any unhealthy activity is ambiguous, since actions that shorten life mean less use of Social Security and Medicare.[7] And the externality logic, if applied consistently, has implications that society is likely to find awkward. For example, any choice that lowers one's income causes a negative externality, since lower income means lower tax payments. This means that someone who decides to be public-interest lawyer rather than a high-priced corporate attorney is imposing an externality.

Even granting that drug use can cause substantial externalities, the mere existence of externalities does not by itself justify policies to reduce drug consumption. The critical question is whether the reduction in externalities achieved by a given intervention exceeds any costs imposed by the intervention itself.

These costs of intervention fall into three main categories. First, there is the loss of utility experienced by those whose consumption the intervention reduces. The fact that certain actions harm third parties does not negate the benefit for the person who engages in the activity. For example, driving a car that generates pollution harms those who live nearby, but it benefits the driver of the car. So, policies that reduce driving both lower pollution and diminish the welfare of drivers. The ideal policy is one that reduces pollution rather than driving per se.

A second cost of policies designed to reduce drug consumption is the direct cost of enforcing the policy. In some cases this is relatively minor; for example, it would not require substantial expenditure to enforce a moderate tax on legalized drugs, since the machinery necessary for collecting such a tax already exists. Likewise, a moderate tax does not provide strong incentives for evasion. Other policies, however, require substantial enforcement expenditure if they are to have a reasonable chance of attaining their stated goal. In particular, prohibition enforcement currently costs about $33 billion per year (Miron 2003b).

The third cost of policies is any indirect consequences generated by the policy. Again, moderate interventions such as a nonprohibitory tax have modest auxiliary consequences; prohibition, in contrast, has the broad range of ancillary effects discussed earlier.[8]

If the costs created by policy exceed the reduction in externalities achieved by the policy, society is better off simply tolerating the externalities. This occurs in many instances. No one attempts to legislate against loud humming on the sidewalk; the negative externalities, while present, are small compared to the costs of attempting to stop them. Drug use has potentially greater externalities, but the costs of attempting to stop drug use are also greater.

Even when policy can reduce externalities by more than any costs created, this rarely involves eliminating the activity. The standard textbook presentation shows that appropriate policy balances the reduction in externalities against the deadweight loss of the policy (e.g., Mankiw 2001: 207–220). For example, driving a car generates pollution, so there is a case for policies that reduce the amount of driving (e.g., taxes on gasoline) or the amount of pollution (e.g., emissions standards). These policies, however, do not prohibit driving; instead, they reduce driving relative to what would otherwise occur. And the conclusion that policies toward externalities involve only a partial reduction in consumption of the externality-generating good is especially relevant if, as seems likely, it is easy to discourage casual drug use that causes minimal externalities but harder to discourage heavy use that generates greater externalities. Alternatively, partial reduction is the best outcome if policy can readily target externality-producing consumption (e.g., that related to drunk driving) as opposed to general consumption (e.g., drinking at home).

A different reason that externalities do not necessarily justify policies to reduce drug use is that reduced drug consumption might translate into increased use of other substances that have similar or greater externalities. For example, as noted above, marijuana appears to impair driving ability less than alcohol, and there is evidence of substitution between the two goods in response to changes in the relative price of the two commodities (DiNardo and Lemieux 2001; Chaloupka and Laixuthai 1994).

Whether or not externalities justify policies to reduce drug consumption, prohibition is almost certainly the wrong approach. Prohibition aims to eliminate all drug consumption rather than targeting externality-causing consumption.[9] Prohibition has enormous enforcement costs and generates huge externalities. Moreover, prohibition has a limited impact on drug consumption and appears to reduce casual rather than heavy consumption (Basov, Jacobson and Miron 2001). The right conclusion, therefore, is that prohibiting drugs does more harm than good, at least with respect to externalities. This does not by itself mean there should be no policies to reduce drug consumption, but these should occur within a regime in which drugs are legal.

Irrational Consumption

A different perspective on drug use is that some consumers are irrational and therefore make inappropriate choices about drug consumption.[10] In particular, myopic consumers might fail to account for the addictiveness and long-term negative consequences that can accompany drug use and therefore consume too much. Under these conditions, policy-induced reductions in drug consumption potentially improve the welfare of myopic consumers.[11]

Some persons undeniably make bad decisions about drugs. As with externalities, however, the harms from drug consumption are often exaggerated and not obviously different from those of other goods.

The first premise of the myopia perspective is that drug use is addictive: consumption today makes one more likely to consume drugs in the future.[12] There is some truth in this view, but existing research suggests drugs are far less addictive than is commonly asserted. Likewise, many legal goods are just as addictive.

One possible measure of addictiveness is the degree to which use continues after initial experimentation. High continued use rates do not necessarily suggest addiction; if people who consume a good find they like it and therefore consume it frequently, the continued use rate is high even if there is no addiction. But addiction does imply a high continued use rate, and this has been used frequently as a measure of addiction.

Table 5.1 presents data on the lifetime, past year, and past month use rates for the major illegal drugs. The data indicate that across all categories of drugs, at most a third of those who have ever used a drug say they have used it in the past year. This does not mean drugs are never addictive, but it fails to suggest a high degree of addictiveness. The fact that continued use rates for marijuana, which is not regarded as physically addictive, are similar to those for crack, which is regarded as highly addictive, also challenges the more extreme claims about addictiveness of drugs.[13] Likewise, the continued use rates for alcohol and tobacco are even higher than those for illegal drugs. And casual observation suggests that continued use rates for other legal goods (e.g., chocolate, caffeine) are perhaps even higher.

A different measure of addictiveness is the degree to which consumers use a particular substance casually or irregularly. The stereo-

Table 5.1

*Illicit drug use in lifetime, past year, and past month
among persons age 12 or older: Percentages, 2002*

Drug	Lifetime	Past Year	Past Month
Any Illicit Drug	46.0	14.9	8.3
Marijuana and Hash	40.4	11.0	6.2
Cocaine	14.4	2.5	0.9
Crack	3.6	0.7	0.2
Heroin	0.16	0.2	0.1
Hallucinogens	14.6	2.0	0.5
LSD	10.4	0.4	0.0
PCP	3.2	0.1	0.0
Inhalants	9.7	0.9	0.3
Tobacco	73.1	36.0	30.4
Alcohol	83.1	66.1	51.0

Source: SAMHSA, Office of Applied Studies,
National Survey on Drug Use and Health, 2002

http://www.samhsa.gov/oas/nhsda/2k2nsduh/html/
Sect1peTabs1to110.htm#tab1.1b,

http://www.samhsa.gov/oas/nhsda/2k2nsduh/html/
Sect2peTabs1to111.htm#tab2.1b accessed 12/12/03

typical depiction of drug addiction suggests that small-scale experimentation progresses inevitably into regular use, and it implies that
occasional or irregular use occurs rarely. In fact, a sizeable percentage of heroin users consume only occasionally, without becoming
heavy users (Zinberg 1979), and measurable withdrawal symptoms
from opioids rarely occur until after several weeks of regular administration (Jaffee 1991: 67).[14] Moreover, the amount of casual or
irregular use under prohibition is not necessarily indicative of what
would occur under legalization. Under prohibition, there are potentially large penalties, both legal and social, for consuming illicit drugs. Thus, those who have only modest demands are likely
to abstain, perhaps choosing licit substances like alcohol instead. If

use were legal, there might more casual use because the legal penalties would be gone and the social penalties would diminish.

Further evidence that addiction is far less important than typical portrayals comes from the experience of returning Vietnam veterans. Robins, Davis, and Nurco (1974) report interviews of veterans eight to twelve months after their return from Vietnam. They find that most addicted veterans gave up their narcotic use voluntarily before departure or after a short, forced treatment period at departure. In subsequent work, Robins et al. (1980) find that although most veterans had access to cheap heroin in Vietnam, only about 35 percent tried it and only about 19 percent became addicted. They also conclude that heroin use does not consistently lead to daily use and addiction, that addiction frequently ceases without treatment, that maintaining recovery from heroin addiction does not require abstention, and that the reason for high levels of social disability among heroin users is likely attributable to characteristics of the users rather than to heroin per se.

Thus, although there is no question that drugs can be addictive, there is also no question that stereotypical characterizations are seriously inaccurate. And the potential for addiction from drugs is not obviously different from that of legal goods such as alcohol, tobacco, caffeine, and myriad other goods.

The second critical assumption underlying the myopia perspective on drug consumption is that consumption harms the drug user. Existing evidence again suggests, however, that the negative consequences of drug use are often overstated.

One possible harm from drug use is diminished health. All drugs carry some health risk, but the degree to which illegal drugs are physically detrimental is far less than generally portrayed, *provided* they are consumed under safe circumstances. The *Merck Manual,* a standard reference book on diagnosis and treatment of diseases (Merck & Co. 1992), states that "people who have developed tolerance [to heroin] may show few signs of drug use and function normally in their usual activities.... Many but not all complications of heroin addiction are related to unsanitary administration of the drug." It also asserts that "there is still little evidence of biologic damage [from marijuana] even among relatively heavy users." Concerning cocaine, the manual does not mention effects of long-term use but emphasizes that all effects, including those that promote aggression, are short-lived. Many of the health risks discussed for all drugs result from overdoses or adulterated doses, not moderate or even heavy levels of use.[15]

A critical problem with standard depictions of the health consequences of drug use is reliance on data sources that are systematically biased toward those who suffer the worst consequences. One example is data from clients of drug treatment programs. Such persons are presumably those who have had the worst experiences with drugs, but this does not indicate the average or typical experience (just as data from alcohol treatment facilities would give a misleading impression of the typical consequences of alcohol consumption). And such information does not illustrate the effect of drug use per se, since such use is often associated with a range of behaviors and characteristics that might be detrimental to health.

Similarly, many discussions fail to distinguish the effects of casual use from those of heavy use or the effects that can occur for some users as opposed to those that usually occur for most users. Moderate doses of over-the-counter medications such as ibuprofen relieve pain effectively for millions of persons each day, but a large dose causes severe damage to the liver. Peanuts are an excellent food source that enhances health for most consumers, yet for persons who are allergic they can be deadly. Standard antibiotics such as penicillin provide relief from moderate to life-threatening diseases for most users but cause illness or death in persons who are allergic. And alcohol in moderation appears to improve rather than diminish health. These examples merely illustrate the general principle that many goods are beneficial in moderation even though potentially harmful in excess; likewise, many goods are beneficial to most persons even though harmful for a few persons. In addition, whatever the health effects of drug consumption, there is no basis for thinking they are more severe than those routinely attributed to numerous legal commodities.

A second alleged harm of drug use is reduced income or likelihood of employment. According to this view, drug use inhibits concentration, coordination, motivation, and other factors that contribute to successful job market experience. For example, widely cited cost-of-illness studies claim that drug use reduces U.S. productivity by tens of billions of dollars per year (Harwood, Fountain, and Livermore 1998). In fact, existing evidence on the relation between drug use and labor market outcomes faces severe methodological difficulties.

The methodological problem is that studies of the relation between drug use and wages utilize individual level data that record both the wages and the drug use of these individuals, along with auxiliary information on demographic and economic characteristics, such as age, education, occupation, or experience. The basic analysis relates wages to drug use and other individual characteristics. The problem is that drug use and wages are both plausibly correlated with unmeasured individual characteristics such as optimism, motivation, sociability, creativity, risk aversion, and the like. Thus, a finding that drug use and wages are correlated can reflect the influence of these omitted characteristics. Stated differently, the standard methodology is not experimental; it does not come from observing the behavior of individuals who have been randomly assigned to different levels of drug use.[16]

The results of existing studies of drug use and wages are therefore difficult to interpret at best. In addition, the results do not consistently support the conclusion that drug use is associated with lower wages. Instead, a persistent puzzle is that drug use is often associated with higher wages.[17] The relation between drug use and certain other labor market outcomes, such as employment status or hours worked, is more frequently found to be negative, but even for these outcomes there are many "paradoxical" results.[18] Given the methodological problems that confront this question, it is not reasonable to conclude from the evidence that drug use *increases* wages or labor supply. But there is certainly no evidence that drug use adversely affects productivity.

Thus, although harm from drug use unquestionably occurs, the magnitude is far more modest than typically portrayed. Moreover, these harms are not inevitable, and they are not obviously different from those of myriad legal goods.

Taking as given that myopia does cause excessive drug consumption in some cases, the mere existence of myopia does not mean attempts to reduce drug consumption are desirable policy; the benefits of reducing irrational consumption must be weighed against the costs of any policy used to achieve that reduction. As with externalities, these costs include reductions in rational consumption, enforcement costs, and any externalities generated by the policy. Further, as with externalities, policy-induced reductions in myopic drug consumption might induce substitution toward goods that have similar or more harmful effects. In addition, prohibition might exacerbate the effects of myopia. Prohibition potentially glamorizes drug use in the eyes of those too shortsighted to consider the long-term consequences. Thus, even if attempts to reduce drug consumption are warranted by myopia, prohibition is unlikely to be the right approach given its huge enforcement costs and negative external effects.[19]

Immoral Consumption

A final perspective on drug consumption is that drug use is evil or immoral, so policy should discourage use to demonstrate society's disapproval.

Economic analysis does not address the morality argument per se. But unless one puts infinite weight on taking a moral stand against drugs, the benefits of making a moral statement must be weighed against the costs of any policy that makes this statement.

Moreover, the analysis earlier shows that, from a moral perspective, prohibition has numerous undesirable effects. Prohibition causes increased violence, some of which affects innocent bystanders caught in drive-by shootings or bomb attacks in Colombia. Prohibition increase the number of children born HIV-infected because it fosters restrictions on the availability of clean needles. Prohibition means that peasants in Latin America, including some who do not grow coca, have their crops destroyed by aerial spraying of pesticides. Prohibition prevents seriously ill patients from using medicines that can alleviate their suffering. And prohibition means that criminals get rich at the expense of society generally.

Thus, from the moral perspective, prohibition is probably the worst choice for addressing the harms related to drugs, given its high enforcement costs and enormous externalities.

Summary

The normative analysis of drug prohibition produces three key conclusions. First, virtually all the effects of prohibition are undesirable, with the possible exception of reduced consumption. Second, reduced drug consumption is not necessarily desirable; any reduction in rational drug consumption is a cost, not a benefit, of policies that reduce drug consumption. Third, even if reduced drug consumption is an appropriate goal for policy, prohibition is almost certainly the wrong approach.

Notes

1. The analysis draws on Miron (2001a).
2. See, for example, Grossman and Chaloupka (1998) on rational cocaine consumption and Chaloupka (1991) and Becker, Grossman, and Murphy (1994) on rational cigarette consumption. Gruber and Koszegi (2001) provide evidence that cigarette consumption is not consistent with the time-consistent version of the rational addiction model, but they also provide evidence of forward-looking behavior by cigarette consumers in

response to announced but not yet implemented tax increases. Viscusi (1994) provides evidence that decisions to smoke are rational in the sense that smokers are risk-taking in many aspects of life.

3. For ease of exposition, this book uses the term "rational" to denote models in which agents form expectations rationally and have time-consistent preferences. This is somewhat at odds with current usage, but it simplifies the exposition considerably.

4. For a more detailed discussion of these issues, see Sullum (2003).

5. See Crancer et al. (1969); Smiley (1986); U.S. Department of Transportation (1993, 1999); Sexton et al. (2000); Fergusson and Horwood (2001), Longo et al. (2000, 2003).

6. See, for example, Behnke and Eyler (1993); Richardson, Day, and McGauhey (1993); U.S. Department of Health and Human Services (1996); Inciardi, Surratt, and Saum (1997); and LaGasse, Seifer, and Lester (1999).

7. Manning et al. (1989) compute the external costs that smokers and drinkers impose on others, concluding that smokers roughly pay their way while drinkers do not. Viscusi (1994) reaches a similar conclusion regarding cigarettes. Evans, Ringel, and Stech (1999) argue that the external costs of cigarettes reported in Manning et al. and Viscusi are understated because they do not include the costs imposed by maternal smoking, which Evans, Ringel, and Stech estimate to be substantial. Their estimates seem problematic on two counts. First, pregnant smokers presumably engaged in a variety of behaviors that might have contributed to outcomes such as low birth weight. Second, it is difficult to know what these smokers would have done had cigarettes not existed. Nevertheless, this discussion illustrates the complexity of such calculations.

8. This is not to say sin taxes are without consequences; see the discussion in Chapter 6.

9. In practice, prohibition does not eliminate consumption; instead, it operates like a sin tax, with a number of additional consequences because the level of the tax is "prohibitive."

10. An alternative formulation of the myopia model is one in which consumers are rational but have time-inconsistent preferences (Laibson 1997; Gruber and Koszegi 2001). For the issues discussed here, the distinction between these formulations is not important. For an alternative view of the literature on myopia, see Cowen (1991).

11. The assumption that policy should attempt to reduce the consequences of myopia raises serious questions about who decides what behavior is "myopic." I do not address this topic here, but that omission is not meant to minimize the importance of this concern.

12. Becker and Murphy (1988) provide a precise definition of addiction.

13. These data are potentially biased by underreporting, and the degree of underreporting with respect to recent use might be greater than with respect to lifetime use. On the other hand, there might be more forgetting of lifetime use than of recent use.

14. Bennett (1986) discusses a literature search and interviews conducted during the early 1980s with opiate users in the United Kingdom. His analysis suggests a modest degree of addictiveness. Few users are pushed into use by sellers; most start with friends or acquaintances. For most it takes months or years to become addicted. Many addicts voluntarily abstain for weeks, months, or years, and many mature out of addiction. The most common reason given for using opiates is that users "like them" and feel their lives are better on opioids. Many use opiates to self-medicate or to follow friends; few exhibited signs of compulsion.

15. Similar evaluations appear elsewhere. These evaluations in no way imply that drug consumption is without risk; indeed, many highlight a range of adverse reactions that can occur as the result of drug use. But they consistently indicate that such reactions are not the norm and that even heavy, regular use can and does occur with modest or minimal negative consequences. See, in particular, Grinspoon and Bakalar (1976) and Morgan and Zimmer (1997) on cocaine; Grinspoon and Bakalar (1993), Hall, Solowij, and Lemon (1994), British Medical Association (1997), and O'Brien (2001) on marijuana; and Trebach (1982) and Zinberg (1979) on heroin.

16. Equivalently, there are no obvious instruments for drug use. Some analyses of this type employ two equation models, with the second having drug use as the dependent variable. The identifying assumptions are implausible, however, and are based mainly on nonlinearities.

17. See, for example, Kaestner (1991, 1994a); Register and Williams (1992); and Gill and Michaels (1992). Kenkel and Ribar (1994) obtain similar results for alcohol consumption.

18. See, for example, Zarkin, French, and Rachal (1992); Kaestner (1994b); and Zarkin et al. (1998).

19. Formal models of myopic (time-inconsistent) consumption do not suggest prohibition; for example, Gruber and Koszegi (2000) provide a model in which the optimal tax rate is finite.

6

Alternatives to Prohibition and Other Policies Toward Drugs

Although not a detailed or complete evaluation of U.S. drug prohibition, the preceding analysis makes a strong case that current policy does more harm than good, even if one takes as given that some reduction in drug consumption is an appropriate goal for public policy. The natural question, therefore, is which policy toward drugs achieves the best balancing of costs and benefits.

In this chapter I address that question. In the first part, I ask whether some variation on prohibition can achieve a better balancing of costs and benefits than current policy. The conclusion is that although certain modifications of prohibition are likely an improvement over current policy, full legalization is better still. In the second part I ask whether, assuming drugs are legal, auxiliary policies toward drugs such as subsidized treatment, needle exchanges, drug testing, or sin taxation are likely to increase economic well-being. The conclusion is that some of these policies might reduce the harms from drug consumption, and legalization combined with these policies is certainly an improvement over prohibition. But these policies generate their own costs, and there is no compelling reason they are better than simply legalizing drugs and treating them like other goods.[1]

Modifications to Current Prohibition

One alternative to current prohibition is a regime with similar laws but a substantially different level of enforcement. Drug arrest rates, drug violation incarceration rates, expenditure on enforcement, asset seizures, and other measures of enforcement have changed substantially over time within the United States and vary widely across countries.[2]

A key consideration in determining the optimal level of enforcement is that such activities likely exhibit decreasing marginal returns in reducing drug consumption. Cost-effective law enforcement addresses the easiest targets first, implying a diminishing marginal effect of enforcement in raising price. Moreover, any increase in price tends to yield diminishing returns in reducing consumption, since casual consumers have cheap substitutes like alcohol and tobacco available and thus relatively elastic demands, while heavy users have less elastic demands. As price rises, the latter group makes up a higher proportion of the market, meaning further increases in price have minimal impact on drug use.

The U.S. experience with alcohol prohibition is consistent with this conjecture. Enforcement increased during the 1920s, but indicators of consumption failed to decline and may actually have risen (Miron and Zwiebel 1991). Part of the explanation could be that illegal supply networks became more efficient over time, but the evidence still suggests that increased enforcement yielded decreasing returns in reducing consumption. Similarly, federal drug enforcement has expanded substantially over the past several decades, yet there is little indication use is lower now than at the beginning of the escalation (Basov, Jacobson, and Miron 2001). And indicators of heavy use, as opposed to any use, show, if anything, increasing trends over the same period.

Thus, whereas many prohibitionists believe present levels of enforcement are "inadequate," there is little evidence that increased enforcement would reduce drug use further. In contrast, decreases in enforcement would reduce violence while leading to only modest increases in consumption, mainly by casual consumers. In the 1950s and 1960s, for example, the resources devoted to prohibition were far smaller than during the last two decades, yet drug-related violence was less common and the consumption of drugs was, if anything, lower than during the 1970s and 1980s. Thus, the net benefit of prohibition plausibly decreases with the degree of enforcement.

A second possible modification of current prohibition is legalization of marijuana only. Many legalization advocates focus on marijuana, and in many places enforcement of marijuana prohibition is less severe than enforcement of prohibition for other drugs. The Netherlands, for example, practices grudging tolerance toward "soft" drugs (e.g., marijuana and hashish) combined with a more punitive approach toward "hard" drugs (e.g., cocaine and heroin).

If the only objective of drug policy is to reduce myopic or externality-causing drug consumption, the case for legalizing marijuana is perhaps stronger than that for legalizing cocaine, opiates, or other illicit drugs. Although the health risks of all these drugs are frequently exaggerated, cocaine, opiates, and other drugs have a greater potential for serious adverse consequences than does marijuana. For example, both cocaine and heroin can cause fatal overdoses, but this outcome is essentially unknown for marijuana.

Nevertheless, the analysis above emphasizes that most negative consequences associated with drugs derive from their prohibition rather than from their consumption. Contrary to popular views, drugs do not differ radically from a range of other commodities, and their distinctive characteristics do not explain the effects of drug prohibition on the market for drugs. The markets for commodities that display similar characteristics but are not prohibited (like cigarettes and coffee) fail to exhibit the features of the market for illicit drugs. Conversely, the markets for commodities that do not display these characteristics but that are often prohibited (like gambling and prostitution) exhibit many of the same negative features as the market for drugs. Thus, the case for legalizing cocaine, heroin, and other hard drugs is as strong as that for marijuana.

A different alternative to current prohibition is decriminalization. As usually defined, decriminalization means eliminating criminal penalties for possession of small amounts of drugs while maintaining penalties against trafficking or possession of larger amounts. Opponents of prohibition usually suggest decriminalization for marijuana. Eleven U.S. states decriminalized marijuana in the 1970s, and a number of European countries have decriminalized marijuana more recently.[3] A few of these countries have also decriminalized other drugs.

Many critics of drug prohibition advocate decriminalization as a superior approach. Decriminalization does reduce the adverse legal consequences of prohibition for users. But because transactions in a decriminalized market are illegal, there is still a black market with all the attendant ills. Thus, decriminalization does not reduce violent crime, improve product quality, eliminate corruption, avoid transfers to criminals, prevent the erosion of civil liberties, or ameliorate most other negatives of prohibition. And it is logically awkward, at a minimum, for society to say that possession and use of drugs are legal but production and sale are not.[4]

This assessment of decriminalization might seem inconsistent with evidence suggesting that drug-related ills are lower in states or countries that have decriminalized one or more drugs. For example, violence rates are lower in countries that have decriminalized than in the United States (Miron 2001). But most of this evidence confuses the effect of decriminalizing drugs with reducing enforcement of all drug laws.[5] Most effects of prohibition depend not just on the existence of this policy but also on the degree to which it is enforced. If decriminalization is also a reduction in enforcement, as no doubt occurs in many places, then its effects are beneficial because it moves policy from prohibition towards legalization. But policy can obtain the benefits of decriminalization by lowering enforcement of trafficking penalties just as well as by scaling back enforcement of possession penalties.

Still a different alternative to prohibition, which might be termed medicalization, is to put control over drugs in the hands of physicians, with little or no oversight from law enforcement. Under current U.S. policy, doctors can prescribe most opiates, cocaine, amphetamines, and depressants, but their ability to prescribe is strictly limited, and they cannot prescribe drugs such as heroin, marijuana, and LSD under any circumstance. More broadly, even when doctors can prescribe controlled substances, they avoid doing so because of concern about legal monitoring of their prescription practices.[6] Under a less restrictive, medical approach, which exists to some degree in Europe, doctors would face minimal legal restraint on their prescribing practices. In particular, they might be allowed to "maintain" addicts by prescribing continued supplies of opiates or other drugs as the "treatment" for addiction.

The critical effect of medicalization is to provide many drug users with a legal supply, thereby reducing the black market. If the restraints on doctors are minimal, some physicians will prescribe freely, potentially reducing the black market to insignificance. Thus, from the perspective of eliminating the negative effects of a prohibition-induced black market, medicalization is beneficial. It is not obvious this approach is better than legalization. If the limits on prescribing are mild, medicalization is little different from de facto legalization. If the limits are strict, substantial numbers of drug consumers will be unable to obtain drugs via medical channels and support the black market instead. The critical issue is that medicalization reduces the degree of enforcement.

Policies Toward Drugs Under Legalization

The discussion so far indicates that although various modifications of prohibition are an improvement over current policy, none is obviously better than simply legalizing drugs. Given this conclusion, the remaining question is whether policy should attempt to ameliorate those negatives consequences of drugs that might occur under legalization. Many such policies already exist, but they are logically separable from the issue of prohibition versus legalization and can potentially continue if drugs are legal.

One policy that might reduce the negative consequences of drug use is government-subsidized drug-abuse treatment. The desired effect of subsidies is to increase the number of persons receiving treatment, thereby reducing the quantity of drug use and especially the adverse effects of drug abuse. The demand for treatment is likely to be drastically lower under legalization; much of the current demand occurs because of pressure applied by prohibition (e.g., court-ordered treatment rather than a jail term for arrestees). But a substantial demand for treatment would remain under legalization.

Subsidizing drug-abuse treatment raises a number of issues. Although it is easy to advocate this policy out of compassion for drug abusers, the question for society is whether the benefits, such as increased earnings for drug users or lower crime committed by users, exceed the costs.[7] Answering this question is difficult because assignment to treatment is not random.[8] Existing evidence, however, does not make a strong case for subsidized treatment (Apsler and Harding 1991). An additional issue is that subsidizing drug treatment might encourage drug use, and even the perception that this occurs—or a feeling by some that subsidizing treatment "rewards" drug use—is a problematic consequence of this policy.

None of these caveats means that treatment never works. The point is that subsidizing treatment is a separate question from whether treatment is beneficial, and it is a separate question from whether prohibition is preferable to legalization. Many critics of prohibition take as given that reduced expenditure for prohibition should translate into increased expenditure for subsidized treatment. It might be desirable to both legalize drugs and subsidize treatment, but subsidized treatment has its own costs and requires independent analysis.

A different way that policy might attempt to reduce the harms of drug use under legalization is via needle exchanges, in which private or government groups provide clean needles to addicts who otherwise share dirty needles and thereby spread HIV and other diseases. There is some evidence these programs reduce needle sharing and little evidence they encourage drug use (Gostin 1991). These programs currently operate in a number of U.S. cities and several foreign countries.[9]

Needle exchanges plausibly reduce the harms associated with drug use, but these programs exist in substantial part because of government restrictions on the sale of clean needles, which in turn reflect prohibition. If drugs were legal there would be far fewer restrictions on nonprescription needle sales. Thus, there is no obvious benefit to such programs under legalization; governments could simply repeal the prohibitions on sales of clean needles, allowing private groups greater freedom to run needle exchanges. In addition, drug prices would be lower under legalization, which would reduce the incentive to inject drugs and thereby diminish any "need" for government needle exchanges. Beyond these considerations, needle exchanges are an awkward activity for the government since they appear to sanction or even subsidize drug use. Even under legalization, this activity is likely to be controversial.

Further policies that might alleviate the harms of drugs under legalization are government media or school-based campaigns that provide information about the consequences of drug use. Other things equal, more information is better, and persuading people not to use drugs circumvents most other issues. But this is not the right benchmark for gauging government anti-drug campaigns. In many cases these exaggerate the dangers of drug use to such a degree that the audience ignores the message entirely. Moreover, existing evidence fails to show that school-based anti-drug campaigns, such as DARE, significantly reduce drug use (see U.S. General Accounting Office 2003 for a review of this literature); likewise, evidence on programs such as the Office of National Drug Control Policy's highly visible media campaign (TV ads linking drug use to terrorism) suggests these programs may even encourage drug use (Hornik et al. 2002).[10] Just as important, accurate information about drugs would be widely accessible in a legal market, so there would be little reason for government intervention in this area.

Yet another policy that is currently employed to ameliorate the negative effects of drug use is government-mandated drug testing. This policy allegedly reduces the frequency of workplace accidents and improves employee productivity. Alternatively, testing can help employers screen out irresponsible or poorly motivated employees. There is nothing wrong with testing per se, but there is no reason for government to mandate this practice. Employers face appropriate incentives to balance the improvement in productivity that might accompany testing against the costs of carrying out the tests. Existing evidence suggests testing can enhance productivity in some instances but in other cases provides limited benefits.[11]

One more policy that might exist in a legalized drug market is restrictions on advertising, such as those currently in effect for tobacco. The assumption behind such policies is that advertising induces people to consume the advertised commodity, but existing evidence does not justify such an assumption. Instead, advertising of mature products mainly affects which brand consumers choose, given they have already decided to consume. In addition, advertising in a legalized market would provide consumers useful information about which substances or consumption methods are less risky, and it would allow firms that innovate in these or other dimensions to attract business by advertising such features. In addition, advertising plausibly raises the costs of the good, as discussed earlier, implying higher prices and lower consumption.

A final way that government might address the harms of drug use within a legalized market is by imposing a tax on drugs in excess of that on other goods. Most economies impose "sin taxes" on various commodities, including tobacco, alcohol, and gasoline. The use of taxes to discourage drug consumption faces an important constraint: the tax must not be so high that it generates a black market. Existing evidence, however, indicates that sin taxes can be substantial without so doing. For example, cigarette taxes in many

European countries account for 75–85 percent of the price (U.S. Department of Health and Human Services 2000).

By reducing consumption, sin taxation potentially reduces externalities and myopic consumption. Whether sin taxation is superior to legalization depends in part on the magnitude of externalities relative to irrational consumption. If drug users impose significant externalities, then sin taxes discourage these externalities and generate revenue that can mitigate the effects. If drug users mainly harm themselves, and if their demands are inelastic, then sin taxes have a limited impact on drug consumption while leaving users less income for food, shelter and clothing. Likewise, sin taxation might mainly deter casual consumption that generates minimal externalities or harm to users. In addition, sin taxation raises political economy issues; political pressures, rather than economics, might determine which commodities are considered sinful.[12] Thus, moderate sin taxation is defensible under certain assumptions but not obviously desirable in practice.

Summary

This chapter has two messages. Although many variations on current prohibition are plausibly beneficial, simple legalization appears even better. Second, within a legalization regime, auxiliary policies might improve welfare, but there is no compelling evidence for any of these interventions.

Notes

1. The analysis draws on Miron and Zwiebel (1995) and Miron (2001a).
2. Becker, Grossman, and Murphy (2003) analyze the positive and normative aspects of prohibition enforcement.
3. The states are Alaska, California, Colorado, Maine, Minnesota, Mississippi, Nebraska, New York, North Carolina, Ohio, and Oregon. Alaska (1990) has since voted to recriminalize, although the implications of that

vote are unclear. A twelfth state, South Dakota, also decriminalized during this period but recriminalized within a year. In 1996 Oregon recriminalized, but in 1998 the voters rescinded recriminalization and returned to decriminalization. More recently, Nevada decriminalized in 2001. See www.norml.org and http://www.drugpolicy.org/statebystate for details. Countries that have decriminalized include Italy (1990), Spain (1992), Portugal (2001), Luxembourg (2001), Belgium (2001), and Austria (1998). Several other countries (The Netherlands, Germany, Denmark, and France, Switzerland, United Kingdom, and Canada) have either de facto decriminalized or are in the process of decriminalizing. See http://eldd.emcdda.eu.int and http://www.norml.org for details.

4. Whether decriminalization would make a substantial difference in the magnitude of the drug consumption depends on the degree to which existing penalties reduce the demand for drugs. Miron (2002) concludes that marijuana decriminalization does not appear to be associated with increased marijuana use, perhaps because decriminalizations mainly ratify de jure what has already occurred de facto.

5. See also Pacula, Chriqui, and King (2003). They argue that the distinction between decriminalizing and non-decriminalizing states is not necessarily important in practice because many non-decriminalizing states lowered penalties and/or enforcement. Thus, comparisons across the two kinds of states are not very powerful.

6. For discussion of these issues, see Hill (1993); American Academy of Pain Medicine and the American Pain Society (1997); Joranson and Gilson (1998); Joranson et al. (2000).

7. Many analyses measure treatment success merely by whether treatment reduces drug use. This is one aspect of treatment, but a complete analysis must consider all the costs and benefits.

8. National Research Council (1999), Chapter 2, and National Research Council (2001), Chapter 8, discuss the scientific issues that arise in attempting to determine the effects of drug treatment. They highlight the virtual absence of studies that include a no-treatment control group. Additional issues in determining cost-effectiveness include the fact that most studies fail to count the time of volunteers and participants in the costs of treatment, that participants in treatment are not a random sample, that participants who stay in treatment are not a random sample of those who enter treatment, that some studies use self-reports of criminal activity, which may be biased, that some "success" of treatment is likely an aging effect, and that participants are in several programs at once, so the appropriate costs are greater than those of any particular program being evaluated.

9. Lurie and Reingold (1993) provide an extensive review of the evidence on needle exchange programs (NEPs) in the United States and abroad. They recognize the standard difficulties in determining the effects of NEPs. The existing evidence does not suggest increased adverse effects from NEPs but also fails to find clear evidence of decreased HIV infection rates. See also National Research Council (1995) for a broader discussion of these issues.

10. Breecher (1972: 197) reports information from Ropp indicating that when coffee was prohibited in Egypt in the sixteenth century, the uproar created interest and increased use. Similarly, he describes the anticigarette laws of the 1920s as significant factors popularizing cigarettes (232). Breecher (1972) also suggests that law enforcement efforts to suppress the amphetamine black market served to advertise the product (Chapter 38); he cites a similar experience in Sweden (Chapter 39). Breecher (1972) further argues that the hysteria surrounding early reports of glue-sniffing, and the subsequent attempts to suppress it, piqued interest and increased this activity (Chapter 44). He suggests a similar phenomenon for LSD (Chapter 50).

11. See National Research Council (1994); Jacobson (2003).

12. See the papers in Shughart (1997) for elaboration of this point.

7 | Conclusion

Prohibition is costly. Direct costs now exceed $33 billion a year, and indirect costs are far greater. Prohibition increases violent and non-violent crime, fosters corruption, and diminishes respect for the law. Prohibition reduces the health and welfare of drug users, subjecting millions whose only crime is drug possession to the risk of arrest and incarceration. Prohibition destroys civil liberties, distorts criminal justice incentives, and inflames racial hostility. Prohibition transfers billions of dollars each year to domestic criminals and enriches foreign revolutionaries who foment terrorism. Prohibition denies medicine to seriously ill patients and prevents doctors from alleviating the pain of the suffering.

It is, of course, true that some people ruin their lives with drugs. The right question for policy analysis, however, is not whether drugs are sometimes misused but whether policy reduces that misuse, and at what cost. The best available evidence shows that prohibition reduces drug use only modestly, and much of this reduction is for casual users rather than "addicts." It is hard to see, therefore, how any benefits from prohibition could possibly outweigh its incredible costs.

Under legalization, there would still be problems related to drugs. Specifically, a small fraction of users would harm themselves and occasionally others, as occurs now for a range of legal goods. Most users, however, would obtain benefits that exceeded any costs, and the enormous externalities imposed by prohibition would disappear.

Critics will claim these conclusions rest on research that is subject to a broad range of caveats: data problems, reverse causation, and the like. This claim is accurate—none of the arguments here "proves" that legalization is better than prohibition. Nevertheless, the arguments and data mustered for legalization are of far greater quality and objectivity than any brought to bear for prohibition. A critical question, therefore, is which side bears the burden of proof?

As a practical matter, inertia and other political forces mean legalizers now bear that burden. Yet there is no reason to give prohibition the benefit of the doubt. American tradition should make legalization—i.e. liberty—the preferred policy, barring compelling evidence prohibition generates benefits in excess of its costs. As I have demonstrated here, a serious weighing of the evidence shows instead that prohibition has enormous costs with, at best, modest and speculative benefits. Liberty and utility thus both recommend that prohibition end now: the goals of prohibition are questionable, the methods are unsound, and the results are deadly.

References

Aaron, Paul, and David Musto. 1981. Temperance and prohibition in America: A historical overview. In *Alcohol and Public Policy: Beyond the Shadow of Prohibition,* ed. Mark H. Moore and Dean R. Gerstein, 127–181. Washington, DC: National Academy Press.

ACLU-Texas. 2003. Too far off task. Report, Austin, TX. http://www.aclutx.org/news/NarcoticsTaskForceReport.pdf.

American Academy of Pain Medicine and the American Pain Society. 1997. The use of opioids for the treatment of chronic pain. *Clinical Journal of Pain* 13: 6–8.

Andelman, David A. 1994. The drug money maze. *Foreign Affairs* 73(4): 94–108.

Anglin, M. Douglas, and George Speckart. 1988. Narcotics use and crime: A multisample, multimethod analysis. *Criminology* 26(2): 197–233.

Apsler, Robert, and Wayne M. Harding. 1991. Cost-effectiveness analysis of drug abuse treatment: Current status and recommendations for future research. In *Drug Abuse Services Research: Background Papers on Drug Abuse Financing and Services Research.* Washington, DC: NIDA. 58–81.

Atkins, Andy. 1998. The economic and political impact of the drug trade and drug control policies in Bolivia. In *Latin American and the Multinational Drug Trade,* ed. Elizabeth Joyce and Carlos Malamud, 97–116. London: Macmillan.

Bagley, Bruce Michael. 1988a. The new Hundred Years War? U.S. national security and the war on drugs in Latin America. *Journal of Interamerican Studies and World Affairs* 30: 161–182.

———. 1988b. Colombia and the war on drugs. *Foreign Affairs* 67: 70–93.

Ball, John C., Lawrence Rosen, John A. Flueck, and David N. Nurco. 1981. The criminality of heroin addicts: When addicted and when off opiates. In *The Drugs-Crime Connection,* ed. James N. Inciardi, 39–65. Beverly

Hills, CA: Sage.

———. 1982. Lifetime criminality of heroin addicts in the United States. *Journal of Drugs Issues* 4: 225–239.

Ball, John C., John W. Shaffer, and David N. Nurco. 1983. The day-to-day criminality of heroin addicts in Baltimore: A study in the continuity of offense rates. *Drug and Alcohol Dependence* 12: 119–142.

Barclay, Gordon, and Cynthia Tavares. 2002. International comparisons of criminal justice statistics 2000. http://www.homeoffice.gov.uk/rds/pdfs2/hosb502.pdf.

Basov, Suren, Mireille Jacobson, and Jeffrey A. Miron. 2001. Prohibition and the market for illegal drugs: An overview of recent history. *World Economics* 2(4): 133–158.

Baum, Dan. 1992. The drug war and civil liberties. *The Nation,* 29 June.

Becker, Gary S., and Kevin M. Murphy. 1988. A theory of rational addiction. *Journal of Political Economy* 96: 675–700.

Becker, Gary S., Michael Grossman, and Kevin M. Murphy. 1994. An empirical analysis of cigarette addiction. *American Economic Review* 84(3): 396–418.

———. 2003. The economic theory of illegal goods: The case of drugs. Unpublished manuscript, University of Chicago.

Behnke, Marylou, and Fonda Davis Eyler. 1993. The consequences of prenatal substance use for the developing fetus, newborn, and young child. *International Journal of the Addictions* 28(13): 1341–1391.

Bennett, Trevor H. 1986. A decision-making approach to opioid addiction. In *The Reasoning Criminal: Rational Choice Perspectives on Offending,* ed. D. Cornish and R. V. G. Clarke, 83–102. New York: Springer-Verlag.

Bennett, Trevor, and Richard Wright. 1984. The relationship between alcohol use and burglary. *British Journal of Addiction* 79: 431–437.

Benson, Bruce L., Iljoong Kim, David W. Rasmussen, and Thomas W. Zuehlke. 1992. Is property crime caused by drug use or by drug enforcement policy? *Applied Economics* 24: 679–692.

Benson, Bruce L. and David W. Rasmussen. 1996. Predatory public finance and the origins of the war on drugs, 1984–1989. *The Independent Review* 1(2): 163–189.

Benson, Bruce L., David W. Rasmussen, and Iljoong Kim. 1998. Deterrence and public policy: Trade-offs in the allocation of police resources. *International Review of Law and Economics* 18: 77–100.

Blumenson, Eric, and Eva Nilsen. 1998. Policing for profit: The drug war's hidden economic agenda. *University of Chicago Law Review* 65: 35-114.

Boudreaux, Donald and Adam Pritchard. 1997. Civil Forfeiture as a Tax. In *Taxing Choice: The Predatory Politics of Fiscal Discrimination*, ed. William Shughart, 347-367. Oakland, CA: Independent Institute.

Breecher, Edward M. 1972. *Licit and Illicit Drugs*. Boston: Little Brown.

British Medical Association. 1997. *Therapeutic Uses of Cannabis.* Dordrecht, The Netherlands: Harwood Academic.

Brown, George F., and Lester P. Silverman. 1974. The retail price of heroin: Estimation and applications. *Journal of the American Statistical Association* 69(347): 595-606.

————. 1980. The retail price of heroin: Estimation and applications. In *Quantitative Explorations in Drug Abuse Policy*, ed. Irving Leveson, 25-53. New York: SP Medical and Scientific Books.

Brumm, Harold J., and Dale O. Cloninger. 1995. The drug war and the homicide rate: A direct correlation? *Cato Journal* 14(3): 507-517.

Bull, Melissa, Don McDowell, Jennifer Norberry, Heather Strang, and Grant Wardlaw. 1992. *Comparative Analysis of Illicit Drug Strategy*. Canberra: Australian Government Publishing Service.

Caulkins, Jonathan P., and Peter Reuter. 1998. What price data tell us about drug markets. *Journal of Drug Issues* 28(3): 593-612.

Chaloupka, Frank J. 1991. Rational addictive behavior and cigarette smoking. *Journal of Political Economy* 99(4): 722-742.

Chaloupka, Frank J., and Adit Laixuthai. 1994. *Do Youths Substitute Alcohol and Marijuana? Some Econometric Evidence*. NBER Working Paper 4662.

Conlin, Michael, Stacy Dickert-Conlin, and John Pepper. 2002. The effect of alcohol prohibition on illicit drug related crimes. Unpublished manuscript, University of Virginia.

Cowen, Tyler. 1991. Self-constraint versus self-liberation. *Ethics* 101: 360-373.

Craig, Richard B. 1981. Colombian narcotics and United States–Colombian relations. *Journal of Interamerican Studies and World Affairs* 23(3): 243-270.

Crancer, Alfred, et al. 1969. Comparison of the effects of marihuana and alcohol on simulated driving performance. *Science* 164: 851-854.

Dawkins, Marvin P. 1997. Drug use and violent crime among adolescents. *Adolescence* 32(126): 395-405.

Dills, Angela, and Jeffrey A. Miron. 2003. Alcohol consumption and alcohol prohibition. *American Law and Economics Review,* forthcoming.

DiNardo, John. 1993. Law enforcement, the price of cocaine, and cocaine use. *Mathematical and Computer Modelling* 17(2): 53–64.

DiNardo, John, and Thomas Lemieux. 2001. Alcohol, marijuana, and American youth: The unintended consequences of government regulation. *Journal of Health Economics* 20: 991–1010.

Duke, Steven B., and Albert C. Gross. 1993. *America's Longest War: Rethinking Our Tragic Crusade Against Drugs.* New York: G.P. Putnam's Sons.

Eckberg, Douglas Lee. 1995. Estimates of early twentieth-century U.S. homicide rates: An econometric approach. *Demography* 32(1): 1–16.

Edwards, Griffith, et. al. 1994. *Alcohol Policy and the Public Good.* New York: Oxford University Press.

Evans, William N., Jeanne S. Ringel, and Diana Stech. 1999. Tobacco taxes and public policy to discourage smoking. In *Tax Policy and the Economy,* ed. James Poterba, 13: 1–55. Cambridge, MA: MIT Press.

Fagan, Jeffrey. 1993. Interactions among drugs, alcohol, and violence. *Journal of Health Affairs* 1: 65–79.

Fajnzylber, Pablo, Daniel Lederman, and Norman Loazya. 1998. *Determinants of Crime Rates in Latin American and the World: An Empirical Assessment.* Washington, DC: World Bank.

———. 1999. Inequality and violent crime. Unpublished manuscript, World Bank.

Falco, Mathea. 1995. Passing grades. *Foreign Affairs* 74(5): 15–20.

Feldman, Herman. 1927. *Prohibition: Its Economic and Industrial Aspects.* New York: Appleton.

Fisher, Irving. 1928. *Prohibition Still at Its Worst.* New York: Alcohol Information Committee.

Friedman, Milton. 1972. Prohibition and Drugs. *Newsweek,* May 1.

———. 1991. The war we are losing. In *Searching for Alternatives: Drug-Control Policy in the United States,* ed. Melvyn B. Krauss and Edward P. Lazear, 53–67. Stanford, CA: Hoover Institution Press.

Gill, Andrew M., and Robert J. Michaels. 1992. Does drug use lower wages? *Industrial and Labor Relations Review* 45(3): 419–434.

Goldstein, Paul J. 1985. The drugs/violence nexus: A tripartite conceptual framework. *Journal of Drug Issues* 15(4): 493–506.

Goldstein, Paul J., Henry H. Brownstein, Patrick J. Ryan, and Patricia A. Bellucci. 1989. Crack and homicide in New York City, 1988: A conceptually based event analysis. *Contemporary Drug Problems* 4: 651–687.

Gordon, Diana R. 1991. Europe's kinder, gentler approach. *The Nation*, 4 February.

Gostin, Larry. 1991. The interconnected epidemic of drug dependency and AIDS. *Harvard Civil Rights/Civil Liberties Law Review* 26: 113–184.

Gray, James P. 2001. *Why Our Drug Laws Have Failed and What We Can Do About It*. Philadelphia: Temple University Press.

Greenberg, Stephanie W., and Freda Adler. 1974. Crime and addiction: An empirical analysis of the literature, 1920–1973. *Contemporary Drug Problems* 3: 221–269.

Greenfeld, Lawrence A. 1998. *Alcohol and Crime: An Analysis of National Data on the Prevalence of Alcohol Involvement in Crime*, Washington, DC: Office of Justice Programs, U.S. Department of Justice.

Grinspoon, Lester, and Bakalar, James B. 1976. *Cocaine: A Drug and Its Social Evolution*. New York: Basic Books.

———. 1993. *Marihuana: The Forbidden Medicine*, New Haven, CT: Yale University Press.

Grossman, Michael, and Frank J. Chaloupka. 1998. The demand for cocaine by young adults: A rational addiction approach. *Journal of Health Economics* 17: 427–474.

Grossman, Michael, Frank Chaloupka, Henry Safer, and Adit Laixuthai. 1993. *Effects of Alcohol Price Policy on Youth*. NBER Working Paper #4385.

Gruber, Jonathan, and Botond Koszegi. 2001. Is addiction "rational"? Theory and evidence. *Quarterly Journal of Economics* 116: 1261–1304.

Hall, Wayne, Nadia Solowij, and Jim Lemon. 1994. *The Health and Psychological Consequences of Cannabis Use*. Canberra: Australia Government Publishing Service.

Harwood, Henrick, Douglas Fountain, and Gina Livermore. 1998. *The Economic Costs of Alcohol and Drug Abuse in the United States, 1992*, Rockville, Maryland: U.S. Department of Health and Human Services.

Haworth, Alan and Ron Simpson, eds. 2004. *Moonshine Markets: Issues in Unrecorded Alcohol Beverage Production and Consumption*, Brunner-Routledge: Florence, Kentucky.

Henneberger, Melinda. It pains a nation of stoics to say 'no' to pain. *New York Times*, April 3, 1994.

Hill, C. Stratton, Jr. 1993. The barriers to adequate pain management with opioid analgesics. *Seminars in Oncology* 20: 1–5.

Hornik, Robert et al. 2002. *Evaluation of the National Youth Anti-Drug*

Media Campaign: Fifth Semi-Annual Report of Findings. Rockville, MD: Westat.

Horowitz, Joel L. 2001. Should the DEA's STRIDE data be used for economic analyses of markets for illegal drugs? *Journal of the American Statistical Association* 96: 1254–1262.

Inciardi, James A., Hilary L. Surratt, and Christine A. Saum. 1997. *Cocaine-Exposed Infants: Social, Legal, and Public Health Issues.* Thousand Oaks, CA: Sage.

Institute of Medicine. 1999. *Marijuana and Medicine: Assessing the Science Base.* Washington, DC: National Academy Press.

Isaac, Paul E. 1965. *Prohibition and Politics: Turbulent Decades in Tennessee, 1885–1920.* Knoxville: University of Tennessee Press.

Jacobson, Mireille. 2003. Drug testing in the trucking industry: The effect on highway safety. *Journal of Law and Economics* 46: 131–156.

Jaffee, Jerome H. 1991. Opiates. In *International Handbook of Addictive Behaviors,* ed. Ilana Glass, 67. London: Tavistock.

Joranson, David E., and Aaron M. Gilson. 1998. Regulatory barriers to pain management. *Seminars in Oncology Nursing* 14(2): 158–163.

Joranson, David E., Karen M. Ryan, Aaron M. Gilson, and June L. Dahl. 2000. Trends in medical use and abuse of opioid analgesics. *Journal of the American Medical Association* 283(13): 1710–1714.

Kaestner, Robert. 1991. The effect of illicit drug use on the wages of young adults. *Journal of Labor Economics* 9(4): 381–412.

———. 1994a. New estimates of the effect of marijuana and cocaine use on wages. *Industrial and Labor Relations Review* 47(3): 454–470.

———. 1994b. The effect of illicit drug use on the labor supply of young adults. *Journal of Human Resources* 29(1): 126–155.

Kaestner, Robert, and Michael Grossman. 1998. The effect of drug use on workplace accidents. *Labour Economics* 5: 267–294.

Kenkel, Donald S., and David C. Ribar. 1994. Alcohol consumption and young adults' socioeconomic status. *Brookings Papers: Microeconomics,* 119–175.

Kolata, Gina. 1999. *Flu: the Great Influenza Pandemic of 1918 and the Search for the Virus That Caused It.* New York: Farrar, Straus & Giroux.

Koper, Christopher S., and Peter Reuter. 1996. Suppressing illegal gun markets: Lessons from drug enforcement. *Law and Contemporary Problems* 59(1): 119–146.

Kuziemko, Ilyana, and Steven D. Levitt. 2003. An empirical analysis of imprisoning drug offenders. *Journal of Public Economics,* forthcoming.

LaGasse, Linda L., Ronald Seifer, and Barry M. Lester. 1999. Interpreting research on prenatal substance exposure in the context of multiple confounding factors. *Clinics in Perinatology* 26(1): 39–54.

Laibson, David I. 1997. Golden eggs and hyperbolic discounting. *Quarterly Journal of Economics* 62: 443–477.

Lerner, Roberto. 1998. The drug trade in Peru. In *Latin America and the Multinational Drug Trade,* ed. Elizabeth Joyce and Carlos Malamud, 117–132. London: Macmillan.

Levitt, Steven D. 2003. Review of *Drug War Heresies* by MacCoun and Reuter. *Journal of Economic Literature* 41: 540–544.

Leung, S. F., and C. E. Phelps. 1993. My kingdom for a drink.... A review of estimates of the price sensitivity of demand for alcoholic beverages. In *Economics and the Prevention of Alcohol-Related Problems: Proceedings of a Workshop on Economic and Socioeconomic Issues in the Prevention of Alcohol-Related Problems,* October 10–11, 1991, ed. M. E. Hilton and G. Bloss, 1–31. Rockville, MD: National Institutes of Health.

Longo, M. C., C. E. Hunger, R. J. Lokan, J. M. White, and M. A. White. 2000. The prevalence of alcohol, cannabinoids, benzodiazepines and stimulants amongst injured drivers and their role in driver culpability: Part II: The relationship between drug prevalence and drug concentration, and driver culpability. *Accident Analysis and Prevention* 32: 623–632.

Longo, M. C., C. E. Hunger, R. J. Lokan, J. M. White, and M. A. White. 2003. The role of alcohol, cannabinoids, benzodiazepines, and stimulants in road crashes. Unpublished manuscript, University of Adelaide.

Lowenfeld, Andreas F. 1989. U.S. law enforcement abroad: The constitution and international law. *American Journal of International Law* 83(4): 880–893.

———. 1990a. U.S. law enforcement abroad: The constitution and international law, continued. *American Journal of International Law* 84(2): 444–493.

———. 1990b. Kidnapping by government order: A follow-up. *American Journal of International Law* 84(3): 712–716.

Lurie, Peter, and Arthur L. Reingold. 1993. *The Public Health Impact of Needle Exchange Programs in the United States and Abroad.* Rockville, MD: Centers of Disease Control.

MacCoun, Robert J., and Peter Reuter. 2001. *Drug War Heresies: Learning from Other Vices, Times and Places.* Cambridge: Cambridge University Press.

Mankiw, N. Gregory. 2001. *Principles of Economics*, 2nd ed. Fort Worth: Harcourt College Publishers.

Manning, Willard G., Linda Blumberg, and Lawrence H. Moulton. 1995. The demand for alcohol: The differential response to price. *Journal of Health Economics* 14: 123–148.

Manning, Willard G. et al. 1989. The taxes of sin: Do smokers and drinkers pay their way? *Journal of the American Medical Association* 261(11): 1604–1609.

Mast, Brent D., Bruce L. Benson, and David W. Rasmussen. 2000. Entrepreneurial police and drug enforcement policy. *Public Choice* 103: 285–308.

McClintock, Cynthia. 1988. The war on drugs: The Peruvian case. *Journal of Interamerican Studies and World Affairs* 30: 127–141.

Melo, Jorge Orlando. 1998. The drug trade, politics, and the economy: The Colombian experience. In *Latin American and the Multinational Drug Trade*, ed. Elizabeth Joyce and Carlos Malamud, 63–96. London: Macmillan.

Merck & Co. 1992. *The Merck Manual of Diagnosis and Therapy*, 16th ed. Rahway, NJ: Merck Research Laboratories.

Merz, Charles. 1931. *The Dry Decade*. Garden City, NY: Doubleday, Doran and Co.

Miron, Jeffrey A. 1998. Drug prohibition. In *The New Palgrave Dictionary of Economics and the Law*, ed. Peter Newman, 648–652. London: Macmillan.

———. 1999. Violence and the U.S. prohibitions of drugs and alcohol. *American Law and Economics Review* 1–2: 78–114.

———. 2001a. The economics of drug prohibition and drug legalization. *Social Research* 68(3): 835–855.

———. 2001b. Violence, guns, and drugs: A cross-country analysis. *Journal of Law and Economics* 44(2): 615–634.

———. 2002. The effect of marijuana decriminalization on the budgets of Massachusetts governments, with a discussion of decriminalization's effect on marijuana use. Report to the Drug Policy Forum of Massachusetts, October 2002.

———. 2003a. Do prohibitions raise prices? Evidence from the markets for cocaine and heroin. *Review of Economics and Statistics* 85(3): 522–530.

———. 2003b. A critique of estimates of the economic costs of drug abuse. Unpublished manuscript, Boston University.

Miron, Jeffrey A., and Jeffrey Zwiebel. 1991. Alcohol consumption during prohibition. *American Economic Review* 81(2): 242–247.

———. 1995. The economic case against drug prohibition. *Journal of Eco-*

nomic Perspectives 9(4): 175–192.

Mishan, E.J. 2001. The staggering costs of drug criminalisation. *Economic Affairs* 21 (1): 37–42.

Moore, Mark H. 1990. Supply reduction and drug law enforcement. In *Drugs and Crime,* ed. Michael Tonry and James Q. Wilson, 109–158. Chicago: University of Chicago Press.

Moore, Mark H., and Dean R. Gerstein, eds. 1981. *Alcohol and Public Policy: Beyond the Shadow of Prohibition.* Washington, DC: National Academy Press.

Morgan, John P. 1982. The Jamaica ginger paralysis. *Journal of the American Medical Association* 245: 1864–1867.

———. 1991. Prohibition is perverse policy: What was true in 1933 is true now. In *Searching for Alternatives: Drug-Control Policy in the United States,* ed. Melvyn B. Krauss and Edward P. Lazear, 405–423. Stanford, CA: Hoover Institution Press.

Morgan, John P., and Lynn Zimmer. 1997. The social pharmacology of smokeable cocaine: Not all it's cracked up to be. In *Crack in America: Demon Drugs and Social Justice,* ed. Craig Reinarman and Harry G. Levine, 131–170. Berkeley: University of California Press.

Musto, David F. 1973. *The American Disease: Origins of Narcotic Control,* New Haven, CT: Yale University Press.

———. 1996. Alcohol in American history. *Scientific American* 4: 78–83.

Nadelmann, Ethan A. 1991. America's drug problem. *Bulletin of the American Academy of Arts and Sciences* XLV(3): 24–40.

National Research Council. 1994. *Under the Influence? Drugs and the American Work Force.* Washington, DC: National Academy Press.

———. 1995. *Preventing HIV Transmission: The Role of Sterile Needles and Bleach.* Washington, DC: National Academy Press.

———. 1999. *Assessment of Two Cost-Effectiveness Studies on Cocaine Control Policy.* Washington, DC: National Academy Press.

National Research Council. 2001. *Informing America's Policy on Illegal Drugs: What We Don't Know Keeps Hurting Us.* Washington, DC: National Academy Press.

O'Brien, Charles P. 2001. Drug addiction and drug abuse. In *Goodman and Gilman's The Pharmacological Basis of Therapeutics,* 10th ed., ed. Joel G. Hardman and Lee E. Limbird, 621–642. New York: McGraw-Hill.

Office of National Drug Control Policy. 2001. *What America's Users Spend on Illegal Drugs.* Washington, DC: Office of National Drug Control Policy.

———. 2003. *The Nation Drug Control Strategy: 2003 Update*. Washington, DC: Office of National Drug Control Policy.

Pacula, Rosalie Liccardo, Jamie F. Chriqui, and Joanna King. 2003. *Marijuana Decriminalization: What Does It Mean in the United States?* NBER Working Paper 9690.

Palmer, David Scott. 1992. Peru, the drug business and the Shining Path: Between Scylla and Charybdis? *Journal of Interamerican Studies and World Affairs* 34(3): 65–88.

Rasmussen, David W., Bruce L. Benson, and David L. Sollars. 1993. Spatial competition in illicit drug markets: The consequences of increased drug law enforcement. *Review of Regional Studies* 23(3): 219–236.

Register, Charles A., and Donald R. Williams. 1992. Labor market effects of marijuana and cocaine use among young men. *Industrial and Labor Relations Review* 45(3): 435–448.

Resignato, Andrew J. 2000. Violent crime: A function of drug use or drug enforcement? *Applied Economics* 32: 681–688.

Reuter, Peter, Mathea Falco, and Robert MacCoun. 1993. *Comparing Western European and North American Drug Policies*. Santa Monica, CA: Rand Corporation.

Reuter, Peter, and Mark A. R. Kleiman. 1986. Risks and prices: An economic analysis of drug enforcement. In *Crime and Justice: An Annual Review of Research*, ed. M. Tonry and M. Norris, 7: 128–179. Chicago: University of Chicago Press.

Richardson, Gale A., Nancy L. Day, and Peggy J. McGauhey. 1993. The impact of prenatal marijuana and cocaine use on the infant and child. *Clinical Obstetrics and Gynecology* 36(2): 302–318.

Robins, Lee N., Darlene H. Davis, and David N. Nurco. 1974. How permanent was Vietnam drug addiction? *American Journal of Public Health* 64: 38–43.

Robins, Lee N., John E. Helzer, Michi Hesselbrock, and Eric Wish. 1980. Vietnam veterans three years after Vietnam: How our study changed our view of heroin. In *The Yearbook of Substance Use and Abuse*, ed. Leon Brill and Charles Winick, 2: 213–230. New York: Human Sciences.

Schlosser, Eric. 1994a. Reefer madness. *Atlantic Monthly*, August.

———. 1994b. Marijuana and the law. *Atlantic Monthly*, September.

Schmeckebier, Laurence F. 1929. *The Bureau of Prohibition: Its History, Activities, and Organization*. Washington, DC: Brookings Institution.

Sexton, B. F., R. J. Tunbridge, N. Brook-Carter, et al. 2000. The influence of cannabis on driving. TRL Report 477 prepared for Road Safety Division, Department of the Environment, Transport and the Regions (U.K.). http://users.wpi.edu/jglavin/TRL477.pdf.

Shephard, Edward M., and Paul Blackley. 2003. Drug enforcement and crime: Recent evidence from New York state. Unpublished manuscript, LeMoyne College.

Shughart, William, ed. 1997. *Taxing Choice: The Predatory Politics of Fiscal Discrimination*. Oakland, CA: Independent Institute.

Silverman, Lester P., and Nancy L. Spruill. 1977. Urban crime and the price of heroin. *Journal of Urban Economics* 4: 80–103.

Smiley, Alison. 1986. Marijuana: On-road and driving simulator studies. *Alcohol, Drugs, and Driving* 2(3–4): 121–134.

Sollars, David L., Bruce L. Benson, and David W. Rasmussen. 1994. Drug enforcement and deterrence of property crime among local jurisdictions. *Public Finance Quarterly* 22: 22–45.

Sullum, Jacob. 1997. No relief in sight. *Reason* 28: 22–29.

———. 2003. *Saying Yes: In Defense of Drug Use*. New York: Jeremy P. Tarcher/Putnam.

Terry, Charles E., and Mildred Pellens. 1928. *The Opium Problem*. Montclair, NJ: Pattern Smith.

Thoumi, Francisco E. 1995. *Political Economy and Illegal Drugs in Colombia*. Boulder, CO: Lynne Rienner.

Tokatlian, Juan G. 1988. National security and drugs: Their impact on Colombian–U.S. relations. *Journal of Interamerican Studies and World Affairs* 30: 133–160.

Toro, María Celia. 1995. *Mexico's "War" on Drugs: Causes and Consequences*. Boulder, CO: Lynne Rienner.

———. 1998. The political repercussions of drug trafficking in Mexico. In *Latin American and the Multinational Drug Trade*, ed. Elizabeth Joyce and Carlos Malamud, 133–148. London: Macmillan.

Trebach, Arnold S. 1982. *The Heroin Solution*. New Haven, CT: Yale University Press.

United Nations Office on Drugs and Crime. 2003. *Global Illicit Drug Trends*. Vienna: UNDCP Research Section.

U.S. Bureau of the Census. 1975. *Historical Statistics of the United States*. Washington, DC: U.S. Government Printing Office.

U.S. Department of Health and Humans Services. 1996. *Behavioral Studies of Drug-Exposed Offspring: Methodological Issues in Human and Animal Research*. NIDA Research Monograph 164. Rockville, MD: NIDA.

U.S. Department of Health and Humans Services. 2000. *Reducing Tobacco Use: A Report of the Surgeon General, Tobacco Taxation Fact Sheet.* http://www.cdc.gov/tobacco/sgr/sgr_2000/factsheets/factsheets_taxation.htm.

U.S. Department of Justice. 1992. *Drugs, Crime and the Justice System: A National Report for the Bureau of Justice Statistics.* Washington, DC: U.S. Department of Justice.

———. 1999. *Substance Abuse and Treatment, State and Federal Prisoners, 1997.* Bureau of Justice Statistics Special Report, January, NCJ 172871.

———. 2003. *Annual Report 2000: Arrestee Drug Abuse Monitoring.* Washington, DC: National Institutes of Justice.

U.S. Department of Transportation. 1993. *Marijuana and Actual Driving Performance,* Washington, DC: U.S. Department of Transportation.

———. 1999. *Marijuana, Alcohol, and Actual Driving Performance.* Springfield, VA: National Technical Information Service.

U.S. Department of Treasury. 2002. *The National Money Laundering Strategy,* Washington, DC: U.S. Department of Treasury.

U.S. General Accounting Office. 1998. Law Enforcement: Information on Drug-Related Police Corruption. Washington, DC: U.S. General Accounting Office.

———. 2003. Youth Illicit Drug Use Prevention: DARE Long-Term Evaluations and Federal Efforts to Identify Effective Programs. Washington, DC: U.S. General Accounting Office.

U.S. Sentencing Commission. 1991. *Mandatory Minimum Penalties in the Federal Criminal Justice System.* Special Report to Congress, August.

Viscusi, W. Kip. 1994. *Cigarette Taxes and the Social Consequences of Smoking.* NBER Working Paper 4891.

Warburton, Clark. 1932. *The Economic Results of Prohibition.* New York: Columbia University Press.

Wieczorek, William F., John W. Welte, and Ernest L. Abel. 1990. Alcohol, drugs and murder: A study of convicted homicide offenders. *Journal of Criminal Justice* 18: 217–227.

Wisotsky, Steven. 1992. *A Society of Suspects: The War on Drugs and Civil Liberties.* Cato Policy Analysis No. 180.

Yoon, Young-Hee, Hsiao-ye Yi, Bridget F. Grant, and Mary C. Dufour. 2001. Liver Cirrhosis Mortality in the United States, 1970–1998. Surveillance Report 57, U.S. Department of Health and Human Services, National Institute on Alcohol Abuse and Alcoholism. http://www.niaaa.nih.gov/publications/Cirr98.pdf.

Yuan, Yuehong, and Jonathan P. Caulkins. 1998. The effect of variation in high-level domestic drug enforcement on variation in drug prices. *Socio-Economic Planning Sciences* 32(4): 265–276.

Zarkin, Gary A., Thomas A. Mroz, Jeremy W. Bray, and Michael T. French. 1998. The relationship between drug use and labor supply for young men. *Labour Economics* 5: 385–409.

Zarkin, Gary A., Michael T. French, and J. Valley Rachal. 1992. The relationship between illicit drug use and labor supply. Unpublished manuscript, Research Triangle Institute.

Zinberg, Norman E. 1979. Non-addictive opiate use. In *Handbook on Drug Abuse,* cd. Robert L. Dupont, Avram Goldstein, and John O'Donnell, 303–313. Washington, DC: NIDA.

Index

103

About the Author

JEFFREY A. MIRON is Research Fellow at the Independent Institute and Professor of Economics at Boston University. He received a B.A., magna cum laude, from Swarthmore College in 1979 and Ph.D. in economics from M.I.T. in 1984. He has been a Research Fellow for the National Bureau of Economic Research; Associate Professor of Economics, University of Michigan; Associate Editor, *Journal of Money, Credit and Banking*; President, Bastiat Institute; Visiting Scholar, Institut d'Economie Industrielle, Université des Sciences Sociales; and Visiting Professor of Economics, Sloan School of Management, Massachusetts Institute of Technology. From 1992–1998, he was chairman of the Department of Economics at Boston University.

A contributor to many volumes, Professor Miron is author of the books, *The Economics of Seasonal Cycles* and *Casebook for Macroeconomics*. He has published more than 25 scholarly articles in refereed journals and his many popular articles have appeared in such publications as the *Boston Business Journal, Boston Globe, Boston Herald, Columbia Daily Tribune, Economic Times, London Observer, Massachusetts News, Orange County Register,* and *San Diego Union-Tribune*.

INDEPENDENT STUDIES IN POLITICAL ECONOMY

For further information and a catalog of publications, please contact:

THE INDEPENDENT INSTITUTE
100 Swan Way, Oakland, California 94621-1428, U.S.A.
510-632-1366   Fax 510-568-6040   info@independent.org   www.independent.org